THE

ELEMENTARY

COMMODORE-64

THE

ELEMENTARY

COMMODORE-64

By

William B. Sanders, Ph.D.

San Diego State University

Illustrations by
Martin Cannon

8943 Fullbright Avenue
Chatsworth, CA 91311-2750
(213) 709-1202

First Edition
> First Printing January, 1983
> Second Printing April, 1983
> Third Printing June, 1983

Second Edition
> First Printing August, 1983
> Second printing September, 1983

ISBN 0-88190-001-X

Acknowledgements

Several people helped directly or indirectly in the creation of ELEMENTARY COMMODORE-64. First and foremost, I owe a great deal to Eric Goez who taught me and several others how to program. Not only did Eric patiently show how to make the computer do all sorts of wonderful things, but he also sparked the imagination of the group of novices of which I was a member.

Stephen Murri of Commodore, Inc. was extremely helpful. Not only did he supply DATAMOST with a prototype of the COMMODORE-64 which I used until production models were available, Mr. Murri sent all kinds of other information for getting the most out of this new machine. Also of Commodore, Inc., Diane LeBold supplied me with relevant issues of Commodore's magazines, *Power Play* and *Commodore: The Microcomputer Magazine.* All in all, I could not have asked for better support than what Commodore supplied.

Dave Gordon of DATAMOST INC. provided a world of support for the book's production. Marcia Carrozzo edited the manuscript for style and consistency, making the work a good deal clearer. Martin Cannon did the art work in a way that communicated ideas creatively and visually. He gave life to the notion that a picture is worth a thousand words. The rest of the staff at DATAMOST were equally helpful and friendly.

Finally, my wife Eli and sons Billy and David, and even our dog Cassiopea, put up with the inconvenience of a writer in the house. To every one of these people I owe a debt of gratitude, but as in all such efforts, if anything goes wrong, it is only the author who is to blame. Therefore, while I happily give those who assisted credit, any of the book's shortcomings are the sole responsibility of the author.

TABLE OF CONTENTS

Preface

My first formal introduction to the workings of a computer was in 1966. At that time our wise mentor told us that if we learned the lowest level operations of a computer, we would be set for life. As a result of this philosophy, we were taught how to count in binary and make conversions to octal and then to decimal. We wrote code for the computer using only "0's" and "1's"! However, we also learned how to write programs in a language called FORTRAN, a high level language. Compared to the binary and octal code, FORTRAN was easy. The problem was that we never really sat down and programmed at a terminal, and so while we had a terrific theoretical understanding of the workings of computers, we never learned very much about interacting with a computer. (We used punch cards, sent our programs over the telephone lines to a computer at UCLA, and waited a week to get our results. If we had an error, we had to send the entire program back for another try.)

Since that time, both computers and the people who use them have changed. To learn how to use a computer, it is unnecessary to learn everything about how they work or the theory behind their operation. It is true that by having a detailed understanding of the theory and operation of computers one can do more with them, but it is something that does not have to be done at the outset. One can learn how to program, and at a later date learn the more technical details of a computer's operation. After all, most people learn to drive without knowing the intricacies of the internal combustion engine of their automobile.

Another major change in computers has been in the transition from "mainframes" and "terminals" to small individual computers. Your Commodore-64 is not merely a terminal. It is a whole computer. Therefore, you are not dependent on using a piece of a larger computer, but you get the whole thing all to yourself. As a result, you are not subject to a set of policies and regulations for getting "on line" or paying for the time you use. You make your own policies and are the captain of your own computer ship. Therefore, it is unnecessary to spend a lot of time discussing the organizational aspects of accessing the CPU (Central Processing Unit), time-sharing, and all of the other aspects of dealing with a computer several people use simultaneously. We will go right to the heart of the matter, programming YOUR computer.

The purpose of this book is primarily to teach you how to work your computer and program in the language called BASIC. It is ELEMENTARY, and so while you will learn a good deal, don't expect to learn everything about working with your Commodore-64. Once you are finished with this book, you will realize how much more you can do with your computer. The more you learn, the more you will find to learn. However, by following the instructions and keying in the examples, you will learn how to write programs with most of the instructions in the version of BASIC on your Commodore-64.

As a final note, don't expect to learn everything right away. Be patient with yourself and your computer, and you will be amazed at how much you will learn. If you do not understand a command or a procedure, you can always come back to it later. Try different things and play with your programs. Think up different projects you would like your computer to do and then try writing a program to do what you want. By all means, though, do not be afraid to make an attempt. With each step or attempt you will make some progress. While it may be slow at times, the accumulated knowledge will eventually lead to understanding.

CHAPTER 1

Introduction

This book is intended to help you operate your new COMMODORE-64 computer, get started programming and make life easier with your computer. It is not for professional programmers or more advanced applications. It is only the first step, and it is for BEGINNERS on the COMMODORE-64 computer. Everything will be kept on an introductory level but, by the time you are finished, you should be able to write and use programs.

To best use ELEMENTARY COMMODORE-64 it is suggested that you start at the beginning and work your way through step-by-step. I have tried to arrange the book so that each part and section logically follows the one preceding it. Skipping around might result in your not understanding some important aspect of the computer's operation. The only exception to this rule is the last chapter where I have put a number of suggestions for programs you might want to buy in order to help you write programs (called UTILITY PROGRAMS). Also, there are descriptions of programs for doing other things such as business, word processing and so forth. When you're finished with this chapter, it would be a good idea to take a quick peek at some of the programs described in the last chapter to see if any of them fit your needs while you're learning about your COMMO-DORE-64. You don't have to purchase any of them but, depending on your interests and needs, you will find some of them very useful.

The first thing to learn about your computer is that it will not "bite" you. It requires a certain amount of care. There are ways you can destroy disk-ettes, tapes, and information but, by following a few simple rules you should be all right. All of us have used sophisticated electronic equipment, such as our stereos, televisions, and video-tape recorders; and there is a certain amount of care they require. Otherwise, there is no need to fear them. Likewise, your computer is electronic. If you pour water or other liquids on the computer while the power is on, you're likely to damage it. Using reasonable care, go ahead and put it to use. Remember, it is vir-tually impossible to write a program which will harm the hardware (or electronic circuits) in your machine. At worst, one of your programs might erase the information on a tape or diskette. Throughout this book there will be tips about how to do things the right and wrong way but, for the most part, treat your computer as you would your microwave oven, garage door opener or radio - with care but without fear.

At this stage of the game it is unnecessary to learn a lot of computer jargon; some of this jargon is necessary to help you understand how your computer operates. As we go on, more new terms will be introduced but, for the most part the text will be in plain English. Nevertheless, you should know the following just to get started.

HARDWARE

Hardware refers to the machine and all of its electronic parts. Basically, everything from the keyboard to the wires and little black chips in your computer is considered "hardware." You will also hear the term "firmware." This is another type of hardware on which programs are written. Called "proms" or "eproms," these chips have information stored in them just as tapes and disks do. Firmware is either inside your computer or in car-tridges or boards you plug into the back of your COMMODORE-64. A biological analogy of hardware is the physical body, most importantly the brain, and firmware is like "inherent" intelligence or "transplanted" intelligence.

SOFTWARE

Software consists of the programs which tell the computer to do different things. Whatever goes into the computer's memory is software. It is analogous to the mind or ideas. Treating the hardware as the brain, any idea which goes into the hardware is the software. Software is to computers as records are to stereos. Software operates either in Random Access Memory (RAM) or Read Only Memory (ROM) memory. (Firmware is hardware with "burned in" software.)

RAM You may hear people talk about expanding their RAM. This is the part of the computer's memory into which you can enter information in the form of data and programs. The more memory you have, the larger the program and more data you can enter. Think of RAM as a warehouse. When you first turn on your computer, the warehouse is just about empty (it says it has 38911 BASIC BYTES FREE); but as you run programs and enter information, the warehouse begins filling up. The larger the warehouse the more information you can store there, and when it is full, you have to stop. COMMODORE-64's come with 64K of RAM. The "K" for computerists refers to "kilobytes" or "thousands-of-bytes", but the actual number is 1024 bytes. (The new disk storage systems are measured in "megabytes" or "millions-of-bytes" - 102400 bytes to be precise. The next time you're at a cocktail party, mention megabytes and you'll really impress everyone.) For now, all you need to know about "bytes" is that they are a measure of storage in computers. The more bytes, the more room you have. Think of them in the same way you would "gallons," "inches" or "meters" - simply a unit of measure.

ROM   A second type of computer memory is ROM meaning "Read Only Memory." This type of memory is "locked" into your computer's chips. Your COMMODORE-64's programming language, called BASIC, is stored in ROM. The difference between ROM and RAM is that whenever you turn off your computer, all information in RAM evaporates, but ROM keeps all of its information. Don't worry, though, you can save whatever is in RAM on diskettes and tape and get it back. We'll see how that is done later.

Now that you know a few terms and enough not to fear your computer, let's get it cranked up and running. If you already have your computer all hooked up and working properly, you can skip the next section and go directly to the "Power On!" section of this chapter.

Hooking Up Your Commodore-64 and Peripheral Equipment

The LAST thing you should do after reading this section is plug in your COMMODORE-64 and turn it on. Everything else should be done **first**. If you bought your computer without a tape recorder or disk drive, it will work fine, but you will need a Commodore Cassette Unit or a disk drive to save information. If you have just the computer, skip to the section on hooking up your TV set to the computer.

TAPE RECORDER

If you are using a tape recorder, either with or without a disk operating system, hooking it up is quite simple. On your Commodore C2N Cassette Unit is a cable to connect it to the computer. Take the cable and insert it into the slot in the back of your computer that is the smaller of the two on the left side. (Right behind the "4," "5" and "6" keys.) Make sure that it is lined up correctly with the "teeth" in the slot, and do not use excessive force when connecting it. That is all there is to it! Your cassette recorder is now ready to operate. Use ordinary cassette tapes - usually 5 minute tapes are the best.

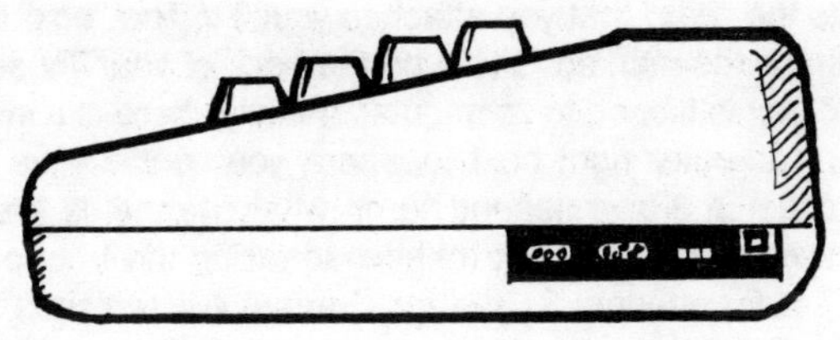

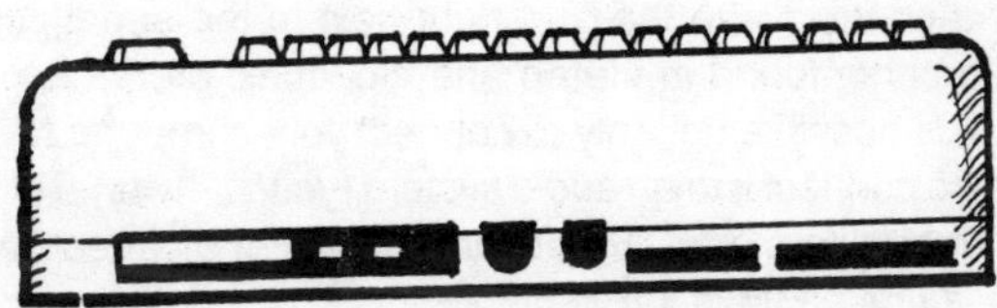

DISK DRIVE

With the COMMODORE-64 you should use the VIC-1541 disk drive. (The VIC-1540 will not operate correctly with the COMMODORE-64 unless you get a special additional chip for it.) To connect your disk drive, attach one end of the disk cable to the serial socket in the back of your computer (the one right next to where the cassette tape recorder is connected behind the "7" and "8" keys) and the other end to the socket in the back of your disk drive, directly above the "fuse." Now plug the power cord for your disk drive into the 3-pronged socket between the on/off switch and the fuse. When everything else is connected, you can plug your disk power cord into a wall socket and flip the switch to ON. Do not do it now. (NOTE: Unlike the cassette tape recorder that draws its power through the computer, the disk drive needs to be plugged into a separate power source.)

TV OR MONITOR

In order to see what's going on in your computer, you need a TV set. On some computers it is necessary to purchase an RF modulator, but your COMMODORE-64 comes with a built-in RF modulator. Just plug one end of the connecting cable that comes with your COMMODORE-64 into the jack in the back of your computer, directly behind the "+" key, and the other end into the "box" that you attach to your TV. The "box" is attached to the antenna leads marked "VHF" on the back of your TV set, and the switch on the box is flipped to "computer." Finally, there is a switch in the back of your computer right next to where you connect the TV cable. Switch it to channel 3 or 4 depending on what channel is "free" in your area. If it is switched to the right (relative to facing the front of your keyboard), it is set for channel 3, and for channel 4 if switched to the left. Then set your TV dial to channel 3 or channel 4. Once that's done you are all set.

Another option you can use with your COMMODORE-64 is a monitor instead of a TV set. Basically, a monitor is the same as a TV except it has higher resolution and is quite useful if you're doing a lot of word processing. To connect to a monitor, you will have to purchase a special connector and cable and connect it to the port right next to the serial port. The 5-Pin DIN audio cable found in stereo and electronic stores is probably a good bet, for it is possible not only to connect your computer to a monitor, but you can also connect it to an audio system (your hi-fi set). The following descriptions of monitors and TV sets are the range of video devices you can use with your COMMODORE-64.

TYPES OF TV SETS

TVs come in a "jillion" different shapes, sizes, etc.; either a color or black and white will work fine. BE CAREFUL in the selection of the TV set you buy! Not all televisions work well with your COMMODORE-64; so ask first before you buy. When I bought my TV set, a color one for the graphics, I simply looked at the color TV's being used on the computers in the stores and bought the same make and model at an "El Cheapo" discount house. An inexpensive way to get clear text is to purchase a black and white set. It has better resolution than a color set, is less expensive, and is good for word processing. Best of all, though, you can get one for as little as $50 and used ones for even less. Whatever the case, check to make sure that the TV set you purchase will work with your COMMODORE-64.

TYPES OF MONITORS

Green Screen — This type of monitor gives a green on black display and can be bought for between $100 and $200. The green and black display is quite good for people doing a lot of word processing and non-graphic programming since it is easy on the eyes. However, since this display presents only green and black, it is not too good for color graphics.

Black and White — This monitor is essentially the same as the green screen, but is in black and white instead of black and green. However, it is more expensive than black and white TV sets, and while it gives better resolution than a television set, the extra cost may not be worth the difference. If you are considering the purchase of a black and white monitor, compare the resolution with a black and white TV set first to see if the extra cost is justified.

Color — This type of monitor is the most expensive, but for people who work a lot with graphics, it is probably worth the added cost. It provides the high resolution for seeing graphics in detail. The very best color monitors require a special interface. Make sure you can get one for your COMMODORE-64 before buying.

PRINTERS

This section simply tells you how to hook up your printer and a little about the different kinds of printers. If your printer is already hooked up and working, take a look at Chapter 9 for tips on maximizing your printer's use.

Types of Printers

There are three basic kinds of printers.

DOT MATRIX — First, the most popular kind of printer is the "dot matrix" printer. This printer has a number of little pins which are fired to form little dots that print out as text or graphics. The advantage of dot matrix printers is their relatively low cost and the fact that many of them can do both text and graphics. The improved quality of text printing of dot matrix printers gives an almost "letter quality" product, and usually can give you several different type faces. In Chapter 9 there are several examples of different printing modes on dot matrix printers. We will be using the VIC-1515 printer by Commodore for most of our examples since it is directly compatible with the COMMODORE-64. (Interfaces for parallel dot-matrix printers are available. See LETTER QUALITY below.)

LETTER QUALITY — Second, for people whose major use of their computer is to do word processing, there are "letter quality" printers. Most of these are "daisy wheel" printers and type characters in much the same way as a typewriter does. Each symbol has a molded image as on typewriter heads. These printers are not good for graphics, but for the user who wants top notch looking letters, manuscripts, reports and other written documents, this type of printer is the best. They tend to be relatively expensive, however, and for most written materials, dot matrix printers are fine. The thing to do before you buy is compare. Special interfaces will be needed to connect a letter quality printer to your COMMODORE-64; so make sure you get a demonstration with the correct interface before buying a printer. Since the COMMODORE-64 has a serial port (instead of a parallel port), you will probably want to get a printer that is serial compatible. However, Xitel, Inc. (2678 North Main Street #1, Walnut Creek, CA 94596, 415-944-9277) makes a parallel interface for the COMMO-DORE-64 which allows you to hook up to a parallel printer.

THERMAL — Third, for those people who are really on a budget, there are "thermal printers." These printers work with a special kind of paper, usually on a roll, and make a "picture" of what is on the computer screen. They can easily handle both text and graphics, but the quality of output is relatively low and the paper is very expensive. The best feature of these printers is their small size and light weight, and for people who travel with their computers and need print-outs, they can be handy. Like dot-matrix and letter quality printers, however, make sure you can interface it to your COMMODORE-64 before purchase.

FREE ADVICE

Before you buy a printer, decide what you will need it for and then look at the features of the different kinds before buying!!! And by all means, ask to see a demonstration on a COMMODORE-64. Never let a salesperson convince you a certain printer will work without seeing a demonstration. Even a salesperson with the best intentions (e.g. they think a certain printer is the best for your needs) may not realize that the model cannot be interfaced to your machine. Only a demonstration is sufficient to remove all doubts!

If you purchase a VIC-1515 or similar Commodore printer, connecting it is very simple. If you have a disk system, connect one end of the cable to the empty slot in the back of the disk drive and the other to the printer. This is called "daisy chaining" the printer. If you do not have a disk drive, connect the cable to the jack next to where the cassette tape cable is connected in the back of your computer. (The same jack where you would connect your disk drive.) In the back of the printer is a switch that can be flipped to "T," "5," or "4." Flip the switch to "4." (The "T" position is for "test" and the "5" position is for identifying the device as "device 5." We will be using the printer as "device 4" in our examples, so switch it to position "4.")

CAUTION
NEVER insert or remove cables or interfaces to your computer while the POWER IS ON! Even if you are rich and can afford to buy new chips every time you blow them by messing with the hardware on your COMMODORE-64 while the power is on, you might give yourself the SHOCK of a lifetime by doing so.

Other Gadgets

Besides the disk drive, TV/monitor, and printer, most new users do not have anything else to hook up at this point, so you can skip on to the next section. However, if you plan on expanding your COMMODORE-64 or have other gadgets you bought with your system, you had better read the following section.

Many Ports of Call

The nicest feature of the COMMODORE-64 is its expandability and adaptability. The various ports and slots on your computer can be used to add many different devices to enhance your system.

MODEM — A MODEM is a device which allows your computer to communicate with other computers over telephone lines. These devices usually require that you hook up your telephone to a part of the modem, or place the phone in an acoustic sender/receiver. The VICMODEM can be used with the COMMODORE-64 simply by inserting it into the "User Port," right next to the cassette port and connecting your telephone line to it. Not only can the modem be used to call up computer bulletin boards, but you can access such information centers as The Source to get everything from weather reports to airline tickets! The only modification needed to use this inexpensive modem is to remove line 400 in the listing in the manual that comes with the VICMODEM.

Z-80 CP/M — This cartridge goes right into the cartridge slot to turn your machine into a Z-80 based computer enabling you to access the vast array of CP/M software. With over 2000 CP/M software programs available, there is little you will not be able to access.

More Wonderful Gadgets — There are numerous other cartridges and interfaces to make the COMMODORE-64 into a multi-faceted machine. Special interfaces will allow you to access and use a variety of peripherals such as various disk drive systems, printers and devices made for other computers. So while the COMMODORE-64 is a terrific microcomputer all by itself, it is fully expandable to make it even better.

POWER ON!

System Check-out

Now that you have your COMMODORE-64 all set to go, you simply plug it in, along with your TV or monitor, disk drive and printer, turn on the power and let her rip! On the right-hand side, next to the port where your power supply cord goes, is a switch. Turn it to the ON position and turn on your TV set. If everything is connected, your TV screen will display the following:

**** COMMODORE 64 BASIC V2 ***

64K RAM SYSTEM 38911 BASIC BYTES FREE

READY.

If you have a color TV, the letters will be in light blue against a dark blue background and a light blue border. Directly below the READY. message is a little blinking square. It is called the "cursor," indicating your computer is waiting for you to press some keys and tell it what to do. Press the RETURN key several times and the cursor will move down the side of the screen. The message on top will scroll off the top of your screen. Your cursor is now at the bottom of the screen. To get it to the top, press the key marked CLR/HOME in the upper right hand corner of your keyboard. Now the cursor will pop to the upper left hand corner. That done, you know your keyboard and computer are all set. We will return to the keyboard in a bit, but first, let's check out your printer, disk drive and/or cassette tape recorder.

To see if your printer is working correctly, put in the following program EXACTLY as it appears below:

First write in the word NEW and press RETURN. (<RETURN> means press the button marked "RETURN.")

```
10 OPEN7,4 <RETURN>
20 PRINT#7, "MY PRINTER IS WORKING!" <RETURN>
30 CLOSE7 <RETURN>
```

Make certain you have written the program as it appears above. If there are even minor differences, change it so that it is precisely the same. Put the ribbon and some paper into your printer. Now, turn on your printer and write in the word RUN on your computer and <RETURN>. If your printer is attached properly, it will print out the message, "MY PRINTER IS WORKING!" If a "SYNTAX ERROR" or some other error message jumps on the screen, it means that you wrote the little test program improperly; so go back and do it again. If the system "hangs up" - the screen goes blank and nothing happens - check to make sure the printer is turned on and the switch on the back is flipped to "4." If it still doesn't work, turn off the power on the printer and computer and review the steps for hooking up your printer.

Booting Disks

Assuming your system is working correctly, let's "boot" a diskette on your VIC-1541 disk drive. (If you have another type of disk system, see the manual that comes with your disk drive.) This will get your Disk Operating System (DOS - pronounced "DAS") operating. Here's how. Turn on your disk drive by flipping the switch located in the back of the drive to the ON position. The red light will light and some noises will come out for a second and then the red light will go off and the green light will come on. At this point insert a *BLANK SOFT SECTORED* diskette (NOT the TEST/DEMO diskette that comes with your drive) with the little square notch oriented to the left with the disk label facing upwards. Now close the door on the disk drive until it clicks shut. At this point you can format your diskette.

(NOTE: Once a disk is formatted, you should NOT format it again unless you want to remove *all* programs from the diskette.) Enter the following:

```
OPEN15,8,15 <RETURN>
PRINT#15, "N0:MYDISK,20" <RETURN>
```

The disk will whirl around for a while and eventually stop. At this point you must "initialize" your diskette. To do so enter the following:

```
PRINT#15, "I0" <RETURN>
```

Now you are all set. Each time you put a disk into your drive, you must initialize it with the above command. Once a diskette is *formatted* with the "N0:" (N is for NEW, but not the same "NEW" that is used to clear your computer's memory!), you need not do it again. However, you must *initialize* the diskette each time you put it into the drive.

WARNING!!

The term "initialize" on your COMMODORE drive means to "get it ready for use." On other computers, "initialize" means to "format" the diskette. Remember, only format a diskette once, but initialize it every time you put it into the drive. "Initializing" your diskette on your COMMODORE drive will not erase any programs. "Formatting" with the "N" command will erase programs! If you have a "write protect" tab covering the notch in your diskette, it will protect the programs on that diskette from accidental erasure. A "write-protected" diskette cannot be formatted or overwritten; so if you have a diskette you do not want ruined, make sure it has a write-protect tab over the notch. *Never* format your TEST/DEMO diskette which comes with your disk drive.

To see if everything is working correctly, enter the following:

```
LOAD "$",8 <RETURN>
```

When the red light goes off, enter

```
LIST <RETURN>
```

Now you should see the name of your diskette displayed. As you add programs to your diskette, they will be added to the directory and listed when you enter the "$" command as shown above and LIST. (See Chapter 9 for more details on using your disk system.)

To retrieve a program from disk, simply LOAD it, and then RUN it. Using your TEST/DEMO diskette, load one of the programs by entering the following:

```
LOAD "<PROGRAM NAME>",8
```

Your screen will first indicate it is searching for the program and then loading it. When you are prompted with "READY.", simply enter

```
RUN <RETURN>
```

to execute the program.

LOADing And RUNning Programs From Tape

The procedure for loading and running programs from tape is quite simple. The following steps show you how:

STEP 1. Make sure your tape recorder is connected and rewind it to the beginning. If you have a tape with programs on it, use it to test loading. (A game cassette <not cartridge> will work fine.) If you do not have a tape with a program on it, enter the following program:

```
NEW <RETURN>
10 PRINT "<YOUR NAME>" <RETURN>
20 END <RETURN>
SAVE "ME" <RETURN>
```

Rewind tape and press REC and PLAY keys simultaneously on your recorder. When the recorder stops and the READY. prompt comes on your TV screen, press STOP and rewind your tape.

STEP 2. Turn on your computer and when you get the cursor, write in the following:

LOAD "<PROGRAM NAME>" <RETURN>

STEP 3. Press the PLAY button on your tape recorder as your computer will prompt you to do. At this point the screen will go blank for a while, and when it reappears you will see the messages

SEARCHING FOR <NAME OF PROGRAM>
FOUND <NAME OF PROGRAM>
<PRESS THE COMMODORE KEY - LOWER LEFT HAND
CORNER OF YOUR KEYBOARD>

The screen will go blank again for a while and when it reappears the second time it will read,

LOADING
READY.

STEP 4. At this point your program is all loaded and ready to go. Enter the word RUN, and your program will then execute. If you used our example program, your name will simply be printed on the screen. Rewind your tape now so that it will be ready for the next time.

(NOTE: On the COMMODORE-64 it is necessary to press the COM-MODORE key during the loading process. Your cassette manual may not mention that fact since your computer may be newer than the latest version of the recorder's manual.)

TAPE TO DISK TRANSFER

If you have both a tape and disk system and you don't want to wait for the longer loading time of tapes every time you run it (especially when you start accumulating several programs on tape), why not transfer your tape files to disk? Just boot your DOS, put a formatted disk into the drive, initialize it, and then load your program on tape. Once your tape program is loaded, simply write in SAVE "<name of file>",8 and now your tape program is on disk! Makes life simpler.

CARTRIDGE PROGRAMS

When you purchase cartridge programs for your computer, simply insert the cartridge into the cartridge port and turn on your computer. It will automatically run the program for you.

The Commodore-64 Keyboard

Almost Like a Typewriter: The Familiar Keys

If you are familiar with a typewriter keyboard, you will see most of the same keys on your COMMODORE-64. For the most part, they do almost the same thing as your typewriter keys. If you type in the word COMPUTER, hitting the same keys you would on a typewriter, the word "COMPUTER" appears on the screen just as it would on paper in a typewriter. However, the upper-case (capital letters) and lower-case letters do not work exactly the same as a typewriter. On the COMMODORE-64, you have to shift into the "upper/lower-case" mode by pressing the "Commodore Key" (the little one in the lower left hand corner with the Commodore logo on it) and the SHIFT key simultaneously. When you do that, your keys will work more like a typewriter. When you want upper-case, simply press the SHIFT key and a letter to get upper-case as you would on a typewriter. Also, the screen has only 40 columns instead of 80 like most typewriters. Of course, you cannot type just anything on the screen. If you start typing away, you'll get a SYNTAX ERROR every time you press RETURN unless you put in the proper commands. Otherwise, though, think of your keyboard as you would a typewriter keyboard. (NOTE: In most of the programming examples, we will be using upper-case only.)

While most of the keys on your COMMODORE-64 look like those on a typewriter, many do not and they are important to know about. The following keys are peculiar to your computer; you will soon get used to them even though they will be a bit mysterious at first:

COMMODORE KEY {Commodore Logo} — This key, located in the lower lefthand corner of your keyboard, is used for shifting between upper case only and upper/lower case (with SHIFT key) and for printing the left hand graphics on the keys. Press the COMMODORE key and the "S" key simultaneously. Instead of getting an "S" you will get a checkerboard on your screen.

CTRL (Control) — In the upper left hand corner of your keyboard is the CTRL key, called the "control key." By pressing the CTRL key and one of the color keys (keys with numbers 1 through 8) you are able to change the colors on the screen. Try holding the CTRL key down and pressing the keys with numbers 1 through 8. You will get different colored cursors by doing so. If you press the CTRL key and the "9" key, you will get reverse printing. Try pressing CTRL-9 (the CTRL and 9 keys simultaneously) and then entering some letters. Now try CTRL-9 and then CTRL-3 and press the space bar several times. Using the CTRL key will give you interesting effects. To turn off the reverse effects, simply press RETURN, or CTRL-0. By now you probably realize that the markings on keys 1 through 0 (e.g. BLK on the "1" key) stand for the characteristics you get when you press that key and the CTRL key simultaneously.

RUN/STOP and RESTORE — These two keys are on opposite sides of your keyboard, but they are used together. The RUN/STOP key used by itself will stop a program execution. Using the RUN/STOP key and the RESTORE keys together, you restore your program to the default conditions. For example, if you've been following the examples, you are probably stuck with some other colored cursor than the light blue one we started with. Press the RUN/STOP and and RESTORE keys simultaneously, and your screen will clear and everything will be restored to normal. If you ever get into a jam and your computer "freezes" up, the RUN/STOP and RESTORE keys will un-jam it, and you will not lose the program in memory. Think of them as "panic buttons" or "reset" keys.

CLR/HOME (Clear Home) — In the upper right hand corner is a very important key, the CLR/HOME key. In computer talk, "HOME" refers to placing the cursor in the upper left hand corner of the screen, and CLR (clear) means to clear the screen. To test this key, press the RETURN key several times so that the cursor is at the bottom of the screen. Now press the CLR/HOME key, and the cursor will pop to the top of the screen. Now press SHIFT-CLR/HOME and your screen will clear and the cursor will again be at the top of the screen. (Enter some text on the screen to see the difference between shifted and non-shifted CLR/HOME).

CRSR (Cursor) KEYS — In the lower right hand corner of your keyboard are the cursor keys. They are used to move the cursor around the screen without affecting anything on the screen. The arrows on the keys indicate the shifted and non-shifted direction of the keys. To get used to using them, here's a little exercise. Press SHIFT-CLR/HOME and then place the cursor right in the middle of the screen without using any other keys. If you can do that, you can use the keys fine. When the cursor keys are used within quotation marks in PRINT statements, funny things begin to happen. Your computer is reading the cursor as something to print to the screen. For example, if you enter

> PRINT "{PRESS DOWN CRSR KEY 10 TIMES} HELLO"
> <RETURN>

you will get a series of inverse "Q's" when you press the "CRSR down" key, and when you press RETURN the message "HELLO" will be spaced 10 places below the line on which you entered the command.

RETURN — The RETURN key is something like the carriage return on a typewriter. In fact, you may see it referred to as a "Carriage Return" or "CR" in computer articles. It works in an analogous manner to a typewriter's carriage return, because the cursor bounces back to the lefthand side of the display screen after you press it. However, there are other uses for the RETURN key which will be discovered as you get into programming.

Arrow and Pi keys — In the upper left hand corner of your keyboard is an arrow key which simply prints out a graphic horizontal arrow for prompts in programs. However, the vertical arrow key on the right side of your keyboard does have functions other than graphic display. In the non-shifted position the key is used for exponentials of numbers. For example, enter PRINT 2 ↑ 2 and RETURN. Your screen will print "4," the value of 2 to the second power. Now enter PRINT SHIFT- ↑ <RETURN> and you will get 3.14159265, the value of Pi.

INST/DEL — This key is an "editing key" to INSert or DELete text. In Chapter 2, we will explain how it works.

KEYBOARD GRAPHICS — On the front of most of the keys there are various graphic symbols. These graphics can be accessed by pressing the key with the desired graphics and either the SHIFT key or COMMO-DORE key. The graphics on the right are accessed with the SHIFT key and the ones on the left with the COMMODORE key. (The graphics on the right cannot be directly accessed from the keyboard when in the upper/lower case mode.) See if you can print all of the different graphic characters to the screen using the SHIFT and COMMODORE keys.

FUNCTION KEYS — On the far right side of your keyboard are the "function keys," numbered from "f1" through "f8." These keys can be accessed by special commands from your programs. Since they are more advanced, their use has been reserved for Chapter 10. For the time being, you will not be using them, but if you have some programming experience, you might want to take a look at Chapter 10 to see how they can be accessed and employed in programs.

SOME NEW MEANINGS FOR OLD KEYS — Some of the familiar keys have different meanings for the computer than we usually associate with the key symbols. Many are math symbols you may or may not recognize. In the next chapter, we will illustrate how these keys can be operated and discuss them in detail. For now let's just take a quick look at the math symbols.

SYMBOL	MEANING
+	Add
−	Subtract
*	Multiply (different than conventional)
/	Divide (different than conventional)
↑	Exponentiation

In addition to some of the new representations for math symbols, other keys will be used in a manner in which you are not accustomed. As we go on, we will explain the meanings of these keys, but just to get used to the idea that your COMMODORE-64 has some special meanings for keys we'll show you some more here which will have special meanings later.

SYMBOL	MEANING
$	Used to indicate a string variable.
:	Used to indicate "end of statement" in program.
%	Indicates an integer variable.
?	Can be used as PRINT command.

Don't worry about understanding what all of these symbols do for the time being. Simply be prepared to think in "computer talk" about symbols. As you become familiar with the keyboard and the uses and meanings of these symbols, you will be able to handle them easily, but the first step is to be aware that the different meanings exist.

SUMMARY

This first chapter has been an overview of your new machine. You should now know how to hook up the different parts of your COMMODORE-64 and get it running. Also, you should be able to boot and initialize a disk, CATALOG the contents of a disk, and run a program from disk or tape. You should know some of the basic DOS commands for manipulating files on your diskette. Finally, you should be familiar with the keyboard and know what the cursor means. At this point there is still much to learn, so don't feel badly if you don't understand everything. As we go along, you will pick up more and more, and what may be confusing now, later will become clear. Have faith in yourself and in no time you will be able to do things you never thought possible.

The next chapter will get you started in learning how to program your COMMODORE-64. It is vitally important that you key in and run the sample programs. Also, it is recommended you make changes in them after you have first tried them out to see if you can make them do slightly different things. Both practical and fun (and crazy!) programs are included so that you can see the purpose behind what you will be doing and enjoy it at the same time.

CHAPTER 2

Ladies and Gentlemen, Start Your Engines

Introduction

This chapter will introduce you to writing programs in the language known as BASIC. Commodore-64 BASIC is different from some other versions of the language; if you are already familiar with BASIC, you will find these differences. However, if you are new to the language, then you will find programming in BASIC very simple. To get ready, turn on your computer; when the "READY" sign comes up on your TV, you are all set to begin programming. If something else is on your screen, press the RESTORE and RUN/STOP key simultaneously and key in NEW to clear memory.

Your Very First Command!

PRINT

Probably the most often used command in BASIC is PRINT. Words enclosed in quotation marks following the PRINT command will be printed to your screen, and numbers and variables will be printed if they are preceded by a print command. It is used to command your computer to print output to the screen or printer from within a program or in the Immediate mode. You may well ask what the difference is between the Immediate and Program mode. Let's take a look.

Immediate Mode — The Immediate mode executes a command as soon as you press RETURN. For example, try the following:

PRINT "THIS IS THE IMMEDIATE MODE" <RETURN>

If everything is working correctly, your screen should look like this:

    PRINT "THIS IS THE IMMEDIATE MODE"
    THIS IS THE IMMEDIATE MODE

    READY.

See how easy that was? Now try PRINTing some numbers, but don't put in the quote marks. Try the following:

    PRINT 6 <RETURN>
    PRINT 54321 <RETURN>

As you can see, numbers can be entered without having to use quote marks. As we will see later, the actual value of the number is placed in memory rather than a "picture" of it.

Program Mode — This mode "delays" the execution of the commands until your program is "RUN." All commands which begin with numbers on the left side will be treated as part of a program. Try the following.

    10 PRINT "THIS IS THE PROGRAM MODE" <RETURN> -

nothing happens, right?
Enter the RUN command and your screen should look like this:

    10 PRINT "THIS IS THE PROGRAM MODE"
    RUN
    THIS IS THE PROGRAM MODE

    READY.

Your Very First Program!

Clearing the Screen and Writing Your Name

Let's write a program and learn two new commands. First, the new commands are CLR/HOME and END. The CLR/HOME command clears the screen and places the cursor in the upper left hand corner. The CLR/HOME command is a one key command made by pressing the SHIFT key and CLR/HOME keys at the same time. In the Program Mode, the CLR/HOME appears as a little heart on your TV, entered as PRINT "{CLR/HOME}". Don't worry, though, it will work fine like that. The END command tells the computer to stop executing commands. From the Immediate mode write in the CLR/HOME command to see what happens. Now let's write a program using {CLR/HOME}, END and PRINT. From now on, press the RETURN key at the end of each line. Throughout the rest of the book, I will no longer be putting in <RETURN> except in reference to entries in the Immediate mode.

```
10 PRINT "{CLR/HOME}" : REM A LITTLE HEART WILL
APPEAR ON YOUR SCREEN
20 PRINT "<YOUR NAME>"
30 END
RUN <RETURN>
```

All you should see on the screen is your name, READY. and the blinking cursor. Now we're going to introduce two shortcuts which will save you time in programming and in memory. First, instead of entering new line numbers, it is possible to put multiple commands on the same line by using a colon ":" between commands. Also, instead of typing in PRINT, you can key in a question mark "?". Try the following program to see how this works.

```
10 ? "{CLR/HOME}"
20 ? "<YOUR NAME>" : END
RUN <RETURN>
```

It did exactly the same thing, but you did not have to put in as many lines or write out the word PRINT. Neat, huh? Now, as a rule of thumb, ALWAYS begin your programs with PRINT "{CLR/HOME}". This will help you get into a habit that will pay off later when you're running all kinds of different programs. There will be exceptions to the rule but, for the most part, by beginning your programs with {CLR/HOME}, you will start off with a nice clear screen rather than a cluttered one.

While we're just getting started it will probably be a good idea to use the colon sparingly. This is because it is easier to understand a program with a minimum number of commands in a single line. Later, when you become more adept at writing programs and want to figure out ways to save memory and speed up program execution, you will probably want to use the colon a good deal more. Also, we want to make liberal use of the REM statement. After the computer sees a REM statement in a line, it goes on to the next line number, executing nothing until it comes to a command which can be executed. The REM statement works as a REMark in your program lines so that others will know what you are doing and as a reminder to yourself what you have done. Just to see how it works, let's put it in our little program.

```
10 PRINT "{CLR/HOME}" : REM THIS CLEARS THE SCREEN
20 PRINT "<YOUR NAME>" : END
30 REM THIS MAGNIFICENT PROGRAM WAS CREATED BY
   <YOUR NAME>
```

Now RUN the program and you will see that the REM statements did not affect it at all! However, it is much clearer as to what your program is doing since you can read what the commands do in the program listing.

Setting Up a Program

Using Line Numbers

Now that we've written a little program let's take a look at using line numbers. In your first program we used the line numbers 10, 20 and 30. We could have used line numbers 1, 2 and 3 or 0, 1 and 2 or even 1000, 2000 and 3000. In fact, there is no need at all to have regular intervals between numbers, and line numbers 1, 32 and 1543 would have worked just fine.

However, we usually want to number our programs by 10's starting at 10. You may well ask, "Wouldn't it be easier to number them 1, 2, 3, 4, 5, etc.?" In some ways maybe it would but overall it definitely would not! Here's why. Type in the word LIST <RETURN>, and if your program is still in memory it will appear on the screen. Suppose you want to insert a line between lines 20 and 30 that prints your home address. Rather than re-writing the entire program, you only have to enter a line number with a value between 20 and 30 (such as 25) and enter the line. Let's try it, but *first remove* the END command in line 20.

```
25 PRINT "<YOUR ADDRESS>"
RUN <RETURN>
```

Aha! You now have your name and address printed on the screen. You had to write in only one line instead of retyping the whole program. Now if we had numbered the program by 1's instead of 10's, you would not have been able to do that since there would be no room between lines numbered 2 and 3 as there was between 20 and 30. You would have to rewrite the whole program. Now, with a small program, this would not be much of a problem, but when you start getting into 100 and 1000 line programs, you'll be glad you have space between line numbers!

Listing Your Program

As we just saw, using the word LIST gives us a listing of our program. To make it neat, type in (SHIFT) CLR/HOME and LIST <RETURN>, and you'll get a listing on a clear screen. However, once you start writing longer programs, you won't want to list everything but only portions. Let's examine the options available with the LIST command

WHAT YOU WRITE	WHAT YOU GET
LIST	Lists entire program
LIST 20	Only line 20 is listed (or any line number you choose.)
LIST 20-30	All lines from 20 to 30 inclusive are listed (or any other range of lines you choose).
LIST -40	Lists from the beginning of the program to line 40 (or any other line number chosen).
LIST 40-	Lists from line 40 (or any other line number chosen) to the end of the program.

Try listing different portions of your program with the options available to see what you get. The following commands will give you some examples of the different options:

```
LIST 25
LIST 20-
LIST -20
LIST 25-30
```

WANNA HAVE SOME FUN?

Usually you will want to use the LIST command from the Immediate mode as you write your program. However, you can use it from within a program. Just for fun, add the following line to your program:

    40 LIST

RUN your program and see what happens. Believe it or not, there are some very practical applications we will see in some programs much later in the book. For the time being, though, it's just for fun. Now, back to some serious stuff.

Saving Your Program

Suppose you write a program, get it working perfectly and then turn off your computer. Since the program is stored in the RAM memory, it will go to Never-Never Land, and you will have to write it in again if you want to use it. Fortunately, it is a simple matter to SAVE a program to your diskette. Let's use our program for an example of SAVEing a program to disk. Make sure your program is still in memory by LISTing it and if it is not, re-write it. Make sure a formatted and initialized disk is in the drive and write in the following: (If you are not certain about disk formatting and initialization, review the section covering those items in Chapter 1.)

    SAVE "0:MY PROGRAM",8

The disk will start whirling and the red light will glow on the disk drive. This means the disk drive is writing your program to disk. When the red light goes out, write in LOAD"$",8 and when the READY prompt appears, enter LIST. You will be presented with a directory of the disk. If you see:

    MY PROGRAM

in the directory, that means your program has been successfully saved to disk.

Saving Programs on Tape

To save a program to tape, put a blank cassette in your tape recorder and rewind it. Press the RECORD button and the PLAY button together on your tape recorder and write in SAVE "MY PROGRAM". The tape recorder will start spinning and the message OK will appear on the screen along with the message SAVING MY PROGRAM. When it is done, the READY prompt will reappear on the screen. Your program is now SAVEed to tape. Unlike SAVEing to disk, you do not have to enter a "port number" (e.g. 8) since the Commodore-64 defaults to the cassette drive with the SAVE command.

Retrieving Your Programs

To make sure you have SAVEd a program to disk or tape, completely turn off your Commodore-64 and then turn it on again. Go ahead and do it. Initialize your diskette by entering OPEN 15,8,15 and PRINT#15, "INITIALIZE0". Then LOAD"$",8 and LIST your disk directory. You should be able to see your program (MY PROGRAM) in the directory. Now enter LOAD "0:MY PROGRAM", 8. The disk drive will whirl for a while, and then your program will be loaded and the READY prompt will reappear. LIST and RUN your program to made sure it's the same one you SAVEd. If it is the same, you know you have successfully SAVEd it to disk.

If you have a tape cassette, just press the PLAY button on your recorder and enter LOAD "MY PROGRAM." The tape will whirl looking for the program and then load it, responding with a READY when completed. LIST and RUN it to make sure it's the correct one.

A SAFETY NET

As you begin writing longer programs, every so many lines, you should SAVE your program to disk or tape. In this way, if your dog accidentally trips over your cord and turns off your computer, you won't lose your program and have to shoot the offending pooch. Saves both programs and dogs.

Now that you have SAVEd and LOADed programs, let's look at another neat trick. Remembering you SAVEd your file under the name MY PRO-GRAM, let's change the contents of that file. First, add the following line and then LIST your program:

27 PRINT "<YOUR CITY, STATE & ZIP>"

Your program is now different from the program you SAVEd in the file MY PROGRAM since you have added line 27. Now write in

SAVE "@0:MY PROGRAM", 8 <RETURN>

Clear memory with NEW, LOAD the file MY PROGRAM and LIST it. As you can see, line 27 is now part of MY PROGRAM. To update a program, LOAD it, make any changes you want, and then SAVE it under the same file name using the "@" before the "0". However, BE CAREFUL. No matter what program is in memory, that program will be SAVEd when you enter the SAVE command. Therefore, if your disk has PROGRAM A and you write PROGRAM B and then SAVE it under the title PROGRAM A, it will destroy PROGRAM A and the SAVEd program will actually be PROGRAM B. Also, if you have a really important program, it is a good idea to make a "back-up" file. For example, if you saved your current program under the file names MY PROGRAM and MY PROGRAM BACK-UP, it would have two files with exactly the same program. To really play it safe, save the program on two different diskettes.

I TOLD YOU SO DEPT.

Sooner or later the following will happen to you: You will have several disks or tapes, one of which you want to format or save programs on. You will pick up the wrong diskette or cassette, one with valuable programs on it. There will be no write protect tab on the diskette or cassette, and after you format it or overwrite programs on it and blow away everything you wanted to keep, you will realize your mistake and say, "!&$#"!%&", and kick your dog. You cannot prevent that from happening at least once, believe me. Therefore, to insure that such a mistake is not irreversible, do the following: MAKE BACK-UP's. Take your ORIGINAL and put it somewhere out of reach, and when you accidentally erase a disk or tape, you can make another copy. Remember, if you fail to follow this advice, your dog will have sore ribs. Be kind to your dog.

Using Your Editor: Fixing Mistakes On the Run

The Error Message and Repairing Them

By now you probably entered something and got a ?SYNTAX ERROR, ?SYNTAX ERROR IN 30 (referring to line 30 or any other line where an error is detected) or some other kind of error message, such as REDO FROM START, which told you something was amiss. This occurs in the Immediate mode as soon as you hit RETURN and in the Program mode as soon as you RUN your program. Depending on the error, you will get a different type of message. As we go along, we will see different messages depending on the operation. For now, we will concentrate on how to fix errors in program lines rather than the nature of the errors themselves. This process is referred to as "editing" programs.

Deleting Lines

The simplest type of editing involves inserting and deleting lines. Let's write a program with an error in it and fix it up.

```
NEW<RETURN>
10 PRINT "{CLR/HOME}"
20 PRINT " AS LONG AS SOMETHING CAN"
30 PRINT : "GO WRONG" : REM LINE WITH ERROR
```

```
40 PRINT "IT WILL"
50 END
RUN <RETURN>
```

If the program is written exactly as depicted above you will get a ?SYNTAX
ERROR IN 30. Now write in,

```
30 <RETURN>
LIST <RETURN>
```

What happened to line 30?! You just learned about deleting a line. Whenever you enter a line number and nothing else, you delete the line. We
have already learned how to insert a line; so to fix the program, enter the
following:

```
30 PRINT "GO WRONG"
```

Now run the program. It should work fine. The error was inserting the
colon between the PRINT statement and the words to be printed. Another
way you could have fixed the program was simply to re-enter line 30
correctly without first deleting it, but I wanted to show you how to delete
a line by entering the line number.

Using the Commodore-64 Editor

Within your COMMODORE-64 is a trusty editor. To see how to work with
your editor, we'll write another bad program and fix it. OK, write the following program and RUN it.

```
NEW
10 PRINT "{CLR/HOME}"
20 PRINT "IF I CAN GOOF UP A PROGRAM "
30 PRINT "I CAN" : FIX IT: REM BAD LINE
40 END
RUN <RETURN>
```

All right, you got a ?SYNTAX ERROR IN 30. To repair it, instead of rewriting
line 30 do the following:

STEP 1. LIST your program

STEP 2. Press SHIFT and CRSR (up/down cursor - the left CRSR
key right below the RETURN key) and "walk" the cursor to LINE
30.

STEP 3. Now, using the right CRSR key, "walk" the cursor to the right until it is just to the right of the first colon.

STEP 4. Press the INST/DEL until the colon and quote mark after CAN disappear.

STEP 5. Press the right CRSR key until the cursor is right over the colon. Now press SHIFT INST/DEL and the colon will jump a space to the right.

STEP 6. Now simply enter a quotation mark after the "T" in the word "IT" in the space you INSerTed with your editor. Press RETURN and you're all finished.

Now LIST the program again; Line 30 should now be correct. Now RUN the program. You should have seen the statement, IF I CAN GOOF UP A PROGRAM I CAN FIX IT. Let's learn more about the editor. Put in the following program: (Remember, in COMMODORE-64 BASIC, we can use question marks to replace PRINT statements. If you LIST the program before you run it, you will see that all of the question marks have magically been transformed to PRINT statements.)

```
10 ? "{CLR/HOME}"
20 ? "SOMETIMES I LIKE TO WRITE LONG, LONG, LONG,
LONG LINES " : WHEW!
30 ?"AND SOMETIMES I LIKE SHORT LINES"
40 END
LIST <RETURN> (See what happened to the question marks.)
RUN <RETURN>
```

OK, after you ran the program it went El Bombo. The problem was that we stuck in that WHEW! without a PRINT statement or quote marks after the colon had terminated the line, or, alternatively, a REM statement before WHEW!. To repair it, LIST the program, "walk" the cursor up to line 20 using the CRSR key, and starting at line 20, retrace the line up to where the mistake was made. To make it simple, remove the second quote mark, leave the colon in place, and add a quote mark after the word WHEW!. Since the colon is now inside the quote marks, it will be printed as part of the PRINT statement and be ignored as a line termination statement. Press RETURN. Now RUN the program.

Now let's take a look at a feature of the COMMODORE-64 editor that might cause some problems. Enter the following BUT DO NOT HIT RETURN!!!!:

20 PRINT "I LIKE TO COMPUUUUUUT

Whoops! There's a mistake, but you haven't finished the line. No sweat. Just press (SHIFT) H-CRSR and back the cursor over the multiple "U's" and re-enter it correctly. (H-CRSR is "horizontal CRSR key" and V-CRSR is "vertical CRSR key.") However, you find that when you press the CRSR key, instead of walking the cursor, you get inverse vertical lines or brackets. With the up/down CRSR you get big blue dots and inverse "Q's." What's going on!??

Not so elementary, Watson. As we noted in Chapter 1, the COMMO-DORE-64 gives you the option of printing those inverse characters inside a set of quotation marks, and to make them you have to press the CRSR keys. To make repairs, simply press RETURN and then using the CRSR keys walk up and make the repairs. As you will see, the CRSR keys are now working fine, even inside the quotation marks. (HINT: Let's face it, it would have been a lot easier simply to press the INST/DEL key a bunch of times to get rid of those offending "U's," but then you would never have learned why your CRSR key went nuts inside the quotation marks.)

WATCH OUT FOR 'RUNDY'

After editing with the COMMODORE-64, I have often entered RUN over the READY prompt, ending up with "RUNDY". Of course, instead of having the program RUN, it gives a ?SYNTAX ERROR. On some computers, as soon as you press RETURN, the remaining characters on the line are forgotten if the cursor has not been passed over them. Therefore, if you are used to other kinds of computers, watch out for RUNDY!

More Editing

Let's do a few more things with your editor before going on. We'll practice some more with inserting characters and numbers, but we will also see how to edit groups of characters. So, let's see how we can use the editor to do more with "insertions." Try the following little program:

```
10 PRINT "{CLR/HOME}"
20 PRINT "NOW IS THE TIME FOR ALL GOOD MEN";
30 PRINT "TO COME TO THE AID OF THEIR COUNTRY"
40 END
```

So far so good, but you meant to include women as well as men in line 20. You could retype the entire line, but all you really need to add is AND WOMEN after MEN. Also, it's really boring to have everything in upper case. Let's change the line to include women and make it both upper and lower case:

> STEP 1. Press the "COMMODORE" and SHIFT simultaneously, and everything will go to lower case characters.

> STEP 2. "Walk" the cursor up to the beginning of the LINE 30 using the CRSR keys and then place the cursor to the right of the first quotation mark.

> STEP 3. Press the SHIFT and INST/DEL keys to make enough spaces to include "and women" and enter "and women."

> STEP 4. To make the sentence correct, place the cursor over the "n" in "now" in LINE 20 and press SHIFT and "N" to capitalize the first letter of the sentence.

After these repairs you now have upper and lower case. When you RUN your program it should read:

> Now is the time for all good men and women to come to the aid of their country.

You will save yourself a great deal of time if you use the editor rather than retyping every mistake you make. (You will save yourself even more time using a commercial editor.) Therefore, to practice with it, there are a several pairs of lines below to repair. The first line shows the wrong way and the second line in the pair shows the correct way. Since "little" things can make a big difference, there are a number of changes to be made. However, as you will soon see, those little mistakes are the ones we are most likely to get snagged on. Practice on these examples until you feel comfortable with the editor - time spent now will save you a great deal later.

Editor Practice

```
50 PRINT  TO BE OR NOT TO BE."
50 PRINT "TO BE OR NOT TO BE."
10 PRINT {CLR/HOME}
10 PRINT "{CLR/HOME}"
80 PRINT "A GOOD MAN IS HARD TO FIND"
80 PRINT "A GOOD PERSON IS HARD TO FIND"
40 PRINT "CLR/HOME" PRINT "WE'RE OFF!
40 PRINT "CLR/HOME" : PRINT "WE'RE OFF!"
```

If you fixed all of those lines, you can repair just about anything. Once you get the hang of it, it's quite simple.

ELEMENTARY MATH OPERATIONS

So far all we've just PRINTed out a lot of text, but that isn't too different from having a fancy typewriter. Now, let's do some simple math operations to show you your computer can compute! Enter the following:

        CLR/HOME
        PRINT 2 + 2

This is what your screen should look like now:

        PRINT 2 + 2
        4

Big deal, so the computer can add - so can my $5 calculator and my 7 year old kid. Who said computers are smart? The programmer (you) is who is smart. OK, so let's give it a little tougher problem.

        CLR/HOME
        PRINT 7.87 * 123.65

Still nothing your calculator can't do, but it'd be a little rough on the 7 year old.

As we progress, we can include more and more aspects of mathematical problems. In the next chapter we will see how we can store values in variables and a lot of things that would choke your calculator. For now, though, we'll simply introduce the format of mathematical manipulations. The " + " and " − " signs work just as they do in regular math, and the " × " is replaced by "*" (asterisk) for multiplication and the " ÷ " is replaced by the "/" (slash) for division.

As we begin dealing with more and more complex math, we will need to observe a certain order in which problems are executed. This is called "precedence." Depending on the operations we use, and the results we are attempting to obtain, we will use one order or another. For example, let's suppose we want to multiply the sum of two numbers by a third number - say the sum of 15 and 20 multiplied by 3. If you entered

        3 * 15 + 20

you would get 3 multiplied by 15 with 20 added on. That's not what you wanted. The reason for that is precedence - multiplication precedes addition. To help you remember the precedence, let's write a little program you can run and then play with some math problems in the Immediate mode to see the results and refer to your "Precedence Chart" on the screen. (This little program is quite handy, so save it to disk or tape to be used later.)

```
10 PRINT "{CLR/HOME}"
20 PRINT "1. - (MINUS SIGNS FOR NEGATIVE NUMBERS -
NOT SUBTRACTION)"
30 PRINT "2. ↑ (EXPONENTIATION)"
40 PRINT "3. * / (MULTIPLICATION AND DIVISION)"
50 PRINT "4. + - (ADDITIONS AND SUBTRACTIONS)"
60 PRINT "ALL OTHER PRECEDENCE BEING EQUAL"
70 PRINT "PRECEDENCE IS FROM LEFT TO RIGHT"
80 PRINT "YOUR COMPUTER FIRST EXECUTES"
90 PRINT "THE NUMBERS IN PARENTHESES, WORKING"
100 PRINT "ITS WAY FROM THE INSIDE OUT"
110 PRINT "IN MULTIPLE PARENTHESES."
```

Try some different problems and see if you can get what you want.

Re-ordering Precedence

Once you get the knack of the order in which math operations work, there is a way to simplify organizing math problems. By placing two or more numbers in PARENTHESES, it is possible to move them up in priority. Let's go back to our example of adding 15 and 20 and then multiplying by 3, but this time we will use parentheses.

```
PRINT 3 * (15 + 20)
```

Now since the multiplication sign has precedence over the addition sign, without the parentheses we would have gotten 3 times 15 plus 20. However, since all operations inside parentheses are executed first, your computer FIRST added 15 and 20 and then multiplied the sum by 3. If more than a single set of parentheses is used in an equation, the innermost is executed first, working its way out.

THE PARENTHESES DUNGEON

To help you remember the order in which math operations are executed within parentheses, think of the operations as being locked up in a multi-layer dungeon. Each cell represents the innermost operation with the cells lined up from left to right. Each "prisoner" is an operation surrounded by walls of parentheses. To escape the dungeon, the prisoner must first get out of the innermost cell. Then the prisoner goes to his right and releases any other prisoners in their cells. Next they break out of the "cell-block" and finally out into the open. Unfortunately, since operations are "executed," this is a lethal analogy for our poor escaping "prisoners." Do some of the examples and see if you can come up with a better analogy.

The following examples show you some operations with parentheses.

```
PRINT 20 + 10 * (8 − 4)
PRINT (12.43 + 92) / 3 ↑ (11 − 3)
PRINT 22 * 3.1415 * 22 * 3.1415
PRINT (9 + 3) / (15 − 5)
PRINT − 10 / 2 * ((12 + 7) + (8 − 4))
```

Now try some of these problems in the proper format expected by your computer:

Multiply the sum of 4 , 9 and 20 by 15

Multiply 35 by 35 and the result by pi {SHIFT ↑}. The vertical arrow/pi key is located between the asterisk and RESTORE keys. (You realize that this will compute the area of a circle with a radius of 35. To find the area of any other circle, just change 35 to another value.) Pi {SHIFT ↑} is treated just like any other number you enter, but to save time, you need only a single key. Pretty neat, huh?

Add up the charges on your long distance calls and divide the sum by the number of calls you made. This will give you the average expense of your calls. Remember, though, you have to do this in one set of statements in a single line. Do the same thing with your checkbook for a month to see the average (mean) amount for your checks.

Summary

This chapter has covered the most basic aspects of programming. At this point you should be able to use the editor in your COMMODORE-64 and write commands in the Immediate and Program (deferred) modes. Also, you should be able to manipulate basic math operations. However, we have only just begun to uncover the power of your computer; at this stage we are treating it more as a glorified calculator than a computer. Nevertheless, what we have covered in this chapter is extremely important to understand because it is the foundation upon which your understanding of programming is to be built. If there are parts you do not understand, review them before continuing. If you still do not understand certain operations after a review, don't worry. You will be able to pick them up later. However, it is still important that you try and get everything to do what it is supposed to do and what you want it to do.

The next chapter will take us into the realm of computer programming and increase your understanding of your COMMODORE-64 considerably. If you take it one step at a time, you will be amazed at the power you have at your fingertips and how easy it is to program. Also, we will be leaving the realm of calculator-like commands and getting down to some honest-to-goodness computer work. This is where the fun really begins.

CHAPTER 3

Moving Along

Introduction

In the last chapter we saw how to get started in executing commands in both the Immediate and Program mode. From now on we will concentrate our efforts on building from the foundation set in Chapter 2 in the Program mode - tying various commands together in a program. We will, however, use the Immediate mode to provide simple examples and to give you an idea of how a certain command works. Also, as we learn more and more commands, it would be a good idea if you started saving the example programs on your disk or cassette so that they can be used for review and a quick "look-up" of examples. Use file names that you can recognize, such as VARIABLE EXAMPLE or HOW TO SUBROUTINES, and REMEMBER each file has to have a different name. Be sure to number example file names (e.g. ARRAYS 1, ARRAYS 2, etc.).

Variables

Perhaps the single most important computer function is in variable commands. Basically, a variable is a symbol which can have more than a single value. If we say, for example $X = 10$, we assign the value of 10 to the variable we call "X." Try the following:

```
X = 10 <RETURN>
READY.
PRINT X <RETURN>
```

Your computer responded

```
10
```

Now type in

```
X = 55.7 <RETURN>
READY.
PRINT X <RETURN>
```

This time you got

```
55.7
```

Each time you assign a value to a variable, it will respond with the last assigned value when you PRINT that variable. Now try the following:

```
X = 10 <RETURN>
Y = 15 <RETURN>
PRINT X + Y <RETURN>
```

Your COMMODORE-64 responded with

```
25
```

As you can see, using numbers, variables can be treated in the same way as math problems. However, instead of using the numbers, you use the variables. Now let's try a little program using variables to calculate the area of a circle.

```
10 PRINT "{CLR/HOME}"
20 PI = (SHIFT) ↑ : REM USE THE "PI" CHARACTER RIGHT
NEXT TO THE 'RESTORE' KEY.
30 R = 15 : REM R IS THE RADIUS OF OUR CIRCLE
40 PRINT PI * (R * R) : REM THIS GIVES US PI TIMES THE
SQUARE OF THE RADIUS
50 END
```

When you RUN the program, you will get the area of a circle with a radius of 15. If you change the value of "R" in line 30, it is a simple matter to quickly calculate the area of any circle you want! Since our example "squares" a number, why don't we use our exponential sign " ↑ ". Change line 40 to read:

```
40 PRINT PI * (R ↑ 2) : REM SAME KEY AS THE "PI" SIGN
BUT YOU DON'T SHIFT TO PRINT IT.
```

That saves typing, doesn't it? RUN the program again and see if you get the same results. You should. Also, change the value of R to see the areas of different circles.

Variable Names

When you name a variable, the computer looks only at the first two characters. For example, if you name a variable NUMBER, all your computer is interested in is NU. Try the following:

```
NUMBER = 63
PRINT NU
```

You got 63 even though you only entered the first two characters of the variable you called NUMBER. Now try this next one:

    NUMBER = 123
    PRINT NUDE

The value 123 is printed because the only characters of interest to the computer are still the first two; so even if you undress NUMBER you still get 123!

Now it may seem that the best thing to do is to use variable names with only two characters. While you're getting used to variables, that's probably not a bad idea. However, as you get into more and more sophisticated programs, it helps to use variable names which are descriptive. For example, the following program uses MEAN as a descriptive variable name:

    10 PRINT "{CLR/HOME}"
    20 A = 15 : B = 23 : C = 38
    30 MEAN = (A + B + C) / 3
    40 PRINT MEAN
    50 END

If the above program were a hundred or more lines long, you would know what the variable MEAN does - it calculates a "mean." Now you'd have to be careful not to have another variable named MEATBALL or some other name beginning with "ME", but it would certainly make it easier to understand what it does.

When naming variables do not use "reserved words" (i.e. programming commands) or reserved variables, and do begin variable names with a letter. There are only 3 reserved variables, TI, TI$ and ST. Let's look at some examples of what is and what is not a valid variable name:

> PRINT = 987 (Invalid name since PRINT is a reserved word.)
> R1 = 321 (Valid name since first character is a letter.)
> 1R = 55 (Invalid since first character is not a letter.)
> FORT = 222 (Invalid since variable name contains reserved word FOR.)
> PR = 99 (Valid name even though reserved word PRINT begins with PR, as only part of the reserved word is used in variable name.)
> TO = 983 (Invalid name since TO is a reserved 2 character word).
> TI = 99999999 (Invalid since TI is a reserved variable for time.
> ADFETDCVRRWRDAAF = 10 (Valid name, but really dumb.)

It is also possible to give values to variables using other variables or a combination of variables and numbers. In our example with the variable MEAN we defined it with other variables. Here are some more examples:

> T = A * (B + C)
> N = N + 1
> SUM = X + Y + Z

Types of Variables

Real Variables

So far we've used only "real" or "floating point" variables in our examples. Any variable which begins with a capital letter and does not end with a dollar sign ($) or percentage sign (%) is a real variable. The value for a real variable can be from + or $-2.93873588E\text{-}39$ to + or $-1.70141183E\text{+}38$. The "E" is the scientific notation for very big numbers. For the time being, don't worry about it. But if you get a result with such a letter in a numeric result, get in touch with a math instructor. At this juncture, figure you can enter numbers in their standard format from

0.01 to 999,999,999. (If your checkbook debit or income tax payments have a scientific notation in them, leave the country.) Think of real variables as being able to hold just about any number you would need, along with the decimal fractions.

Integer Variables

Integer variables contain only "integer" or "whole" numbers - ones without fractions. The following are some examples:

```
AB% = 345
K% = R% + N%
ADD% = ADD% + NUM%
WXY% = 88 + LR%
```

The values of integer variables can range from − 32767 to + 32767 and, like real variables, only the first two characters are read. However, the "%" is always read, no matter how many characters are used. So a variable named WA% is the same as WAX%. Also, a variable named ABC is different from one named ABC%; therefore, both variables could be used in the same program and each be considered unique. As they have a lower range than real variables, integer variables have limited applications; however, integer variables take up less memory and execute faster than real variables and so they have many useful applications. They can be used in mathematical operations in the same way as are real variables, but since they do not store fractions, operations using division and similar fraction operations must be done with care. Try some of the following operations from the Immediate mode to see how they work:

```
A% = 15 : B% = 21 : C% = B% + A% : PRINT C% <RETURN>
36
LL% = 17 :JJ% = LL% / 5 : PRINT JJ% <RETURN>
3
Z% = −11 :XY% = Z% + 51 : PRINT XY% <RETURN>
40
```

String Variables

String variables are extremely useful in formatting what you will see on the screen. Like real and integer variables, they are sent to the screen by the PRINT statement. However, rather than printing only numbers, string variables send all kinds of characters, called "strings," to the screen. String variables are indicated by a dollar sign ($) on the end of a variable. For example, A$, BAD$, G$, and PULL$ are all legitimate string variables. (In computer parlance, we use the term "string" for the dollar sign. Thus, our examples would be called "A string," "BAD string," etc.) String variables are defined by placing the "string" in quotation marks, just as we did with other messages we printed out.

Let's try out a few examples from the Immediate mode:

```
ABC$ = "ABC" : PRINT ABC$ <RETURN>
G$ = "BURLESQUE" : PRINT G$ <RETURN>
KAT$ ="CAT" : PRINT KAT$ <RETURN>
NUMBER$ = "123456789" : PRINT NUMBER$ <RETURN>
B1$ = "5 + 10 + 20" : PRINT B1$ <RETURN>
```

In the same way that real and integer variables use only the first two characters, a string variable must begin with a letter and use non-reserved words. More importantly, you probably noticed in our examples that numbers in string variables are not treated as numbers but rather as "words" or "messages." For example, when you PRINTed B1$, instead of printing out "35" (the sum of 5, 10 and 20), B1$ printed out exactly what you put in quotes, 5 + 10 + 20. Do not attempt to do math with string variables. (In later chapters we'll see some tricks to convert string variables to numeric-real or integer- variables, but for now just treat them as messages.)

Now let's put all of our accumulated knowledge together and write a program which uses variables. We will start a little program which will allow you to subtract a check from your checkbook and print the amount. This program will be the beginning of something we will later develop to give you a handy little program with which to do checkbook balancing.

```
10 PRINT "{CLR/HOME}"
20 BALANCE = 571.88 : REM ANY FIGURE WILL DO.
BALANCE (BA) IS A REAL VARIABLE
30 CHECK = 29.95 : REM WHAT YOU LAST SPENT IN THE
COMPUTER STORE. CHECK (CH) IS A REAL VARIABLE.
40 B$ = "YOUR BEGINNING BALANCE IS $"
50 C$ = "YOUR CHECK IS FOR $"
60 NB$ = "YOUR NEW BALANCE IS $": REM B$, C$ AND NB$
ARE STRING VARIABLES
70 PRINT B$;BALANCE
80 PRINT C$;CHECK
90 N = BALANCE - CHECK
100 PRINT NB$; N
110 END
```

Since this is a fairly long program for this stage of the game, make sure you put in everything correctly. For the computer, it is critical that you distinguish between commas, semi-colons, periods, etc. Also save it to disk. To play with it, change the values in lines 20 and 30.

Let's quickly review what we have done.

STEP 1. First we defined the real variables "BALANCE" and "CHECK" (which your COMMODORE-64 read as BA and CH since it cares only about the first two characters.)

STEP 2. Then we defined string variables B$, C$, and NB$ to use as labels in screen formatting.

STEP 3. Finally, we printed out all of our information using our variables with one new variable, "N", defined as the difference between BALANCE and CHECK.

Note how we formatted the "OUTPUT" (what you see on your screen) of our PRINT statements. The semi-colon ";" between the variables accomplished two things: (1) it told the computer where one variable ended and the next began, and (2) it told the computer to PRINT the second variable right after the first one. Thus, it took the string variable NB$

        YOUR NEW BALANCE IS $#

and stuck the value of the real variable N right after the dollar sign (exactly where we placed the hatch #). Later we will go more into the formatting of OUTPUT, but for now let's take a quick look at using punctuation in formatting text. We will use the comma "," and semi-colon ";" and "new line" to illustrate basic formatting. Put in the following little program:

```
NEW <RETURN>
10 PRINT "{CLR/HOME}"
20 A$ = "HERE" : B$ = "THERE" : C$ = "WHERE"
30 PRINT A$; : PRINT B$; : PRINT C$; : REM SEMI-COLONS
35 PRINT
40 PRINT A$, : PRINT B$, : PRINT C$,: REM COMMAS
45 PRINT : REM A 'PRINT' BY ITSELF GIVES A VERTICAL
'SPACE' IN FORMATTING
50 PRINT A$ : PRINT B$ : PRINT C$ : REM 'NEW LINES'
60 END
```

Now RUN the program. As you should see, the little differences in lines 30, 40, and 50 made big differences on the screen. The first set is all crammed together, the second set is spaced evenly across the screen, and the third set is stacked one on top of the other. As we saw in the previous program, semi-colons put numbers and strings right next to one another. However, using commas after a PRINTed variable will space output in groups of four across the screen, and using "new lines" in the form of colons or new line numbers will make the output start on a new line. A PRINT statement all by itself will put a vertical "linefeed" between statements. Try the following little program to see how PRINT statements all by themselves can be used.

```
NEW <RETURN>
10 PRINT "{CLR/HOME}"
20 PRINT "WHENEVER YOU PUT IN A PRINT STATEMENT";
: REM NOTE PLACEMENT OF SEMI-COLON
30 PRINT " ALL BY ITSELF, IT GIVES A 'LINEFEED'."
40 PRINT
50 PRINT "SEE WHAT I MEAN?"
60 END
```

Play with commas, semi-colons, and "new lines" with variables and string variables until you get the hang of it. They are very important and are the source of program "bugs."

BUGS and BOMBS

We've mentioned "bugs" and "bombs" in programs but never really explained what they meant. "Bugs" are simply errors in programs which either create ?SYNTAX ERRORs or prevent your program from doing what you want it to do. "Debugging" is the process of removing "bugs." "Bombing" is what your program does when it encounters a "bug." This is all computer lingo; if you use it in your conversations, people will think you really know a lot about computers or have a bug in your personality.

Input and Output (I/O)

Input and output, often referred to as I/O, are ways of putting things into your computer and getting it out. Usually we put IN information from the keyboard, save it to disk or tape, and then later put it in from the disk drive or cassette recorder. When we want information OUT of the computer, we want it to go to our screen or printer. This is what I/O means. So far, we have entered information IN the computer from the keyboard either in the Program or in the Immediate mode. Using the PRINT statement, we have sent information OUT to the screen. However, there are other ways we can INPUT information with a combination of programming and keyboard commands. Let's look at some of these ways and make our CHECKBOOK program a lot simpler to use.

INPUT

The INPUT command is placed in a program and expects some kind of response from the keyboard and then a RETURN. (A RETURN alone will also work, but the response is read as "".) It must be part of a program and cannot be used from the Immediate mode. (If attempted from the Immediate mode, there will be an ?ILLEGAL DIRECT ERROR message.) Let's look at a simple example:

```
NEW <RETURN>
10 PRINT "{CLR/HOME}"
20 INPUT X : REM 'X' IS A NUMERIC VARIABLE SO ENTER
A NUMBER
30 PRINT X
40 END
```

RUN the program and your screen will go blank and a "?" along with a blinking cursor will sit there until you enter a number and then the computer will PRINT the number you just entered. Really interesting, huh?

Let's try INPUTing the same information but using a slightly different format. The nice thing about INPUT statements is that they have some of the same features as PRINT statements for getting messages on the screen. Look at the following program:

```
NEW <RETURN>
10 PRINT "{CLR/HOME}"
20 INPUT "ENTER YOUR AGE "; X
30 PRINT "{CLR/HOME}" : PRINT : PRINT : PRINT
40 PRINT "YOUR AGE IS "; X
```

Now RUN the program. You will see that the presentation is a little more interesting. Also notice we did not put an END command at the end of the program. In COMMODORE-64 it is not necessary to enter an END command, but it is usually a good idea to do so. As we get into more advanced topics, we will see that our program can jump around, the place we want it to END will be in the middle, and we will need an END statement so that it will not crash into an area we don't want it to go. So, while an END command really has not been necessary up to now, it is nevertheless a good habit to develop.

Let's soup up our program a little more with the INPUT statement.

```
NEW <RETURN>
10 PRINT "{CLR/HOME}"
20 INPUT "ENTER YOUR NAME -> "; NA$
30 PRINT
40 INPUT "ENTER YOUR AGE -> "; AG%
50 PRINT
60 INPUT "PRESS <RETURN> TO CONTINUE "; RT$
70 ? "{CLR/HOME}" : ? : ? : ? : ? : ? : REM USING "?" AS
SUBSTITUTES FOR PRINT
80 PRINT NA$; " IS "; AG% ; " YEARS OLD. " : REM BE CARE-
FUL WHERE YOU PUT YOUR QUOTE MARKS AND SEMI-
COLONS IN THIS LINE
90 END
```

Now we're getting somewhere. You can enter information as numeric or string variables and the OUTPUT is formatted so you know what's going on. As your programs become larger and more complicated, it is very important to connect your string variables and numeric variables in such a way that it is easy to see what the numbers on the screen mean. Let's face it, a computer wouldn't be very helpful if it filled the screen with numbers and you didn't know what they meant! Line 60 is the format for a pause in your program. RT$ doesn't hold any information but since INPUT statements expect something from the keyboard, a variable, RT$ (for RETURN), is as good as any.

GETing Information

The GET statement is something like the INPUT statement, except it is executed as soon as you hit a key. To see how it works, try the following program. You should note that to be of use, GET must be put into a little "loop" routine.

```
NEW <RETURN>
10 PRINT "{CLR/HOME}"
20 ? : ? : ? : ?
30 PRINT " ENTER A NUMBER FROM 1-9 ";
35 GET N: IF N < 1 OR N > 9 THEN 35 : REM NOTE FORMAT
IN THIS LINE
40 ? : ?
50 PRINT " HIT ANY KEY TO CONTINUE ";
55 GET K$: IF K$ = "" THEN 55 : REM USED AS A PAUSE
UNTIL A KEY IS PRESSED
60 ? "{CLR/HOME}" : ? : ? : ? : ?
70 PRINT "YOUR NUMBER IS -->" ; N
80 END
```

Notice that the GET statement is executed as soon as you hit a key. With an INPUT statement you first enter information and then press the RETURN key before the program executes. The good thing about the GET statement is that it is a faster way to enter and execute from the keyboard; the problem is that you can only enter a single character before the program takes off again. If you press the wrong key there is no chance to correct the error before pressing the RETURN key as there is with the INPUT command.

READing In DATA

A third way to enter data into a program is with READ and DATA statements. However, instead of entering the data through the keyboard, DATA in one part of the program is READ in from another part. Each READ statement looks at elements in DATA statements sequentially. The READ command is associated with a variable which looks at the next DATA statement and places the numeric value or string in the variable. Let's look at the following example:

```
NEW <RETURN>
10 PRINT "{CLR/HOME}"
20 READ NA$ : REM READS NAME
30 READ OC$ : REM READS OCCUPATION
40 READ SN : REM READS STREET NUMBER
50 READ ST$ : REM READS STREET NAME
60 READ CT$ : REM READS CITY
70 READ SA$ : REM READS STATE
80 READ ZIP : REM READS ZIP CODE
90 PRINT : PRINT : PRINT
100 REM BEGIN PRINTING OUT WHAT 'READ' READ IN. (BE
CAREFUL TO PUT IN EVERYTHING EXACTLY AS IT IS LISTED.)
110 PRINT NA$
120 PRINT OC$
130 PRINT SN; " "; ST$
140 PRINT CT$ ; ","; SA$ ;" "; ZIP
150 END
1000 DATA DAVID GORDON, SOFTWARE TYCOON, 8943,
FULLBRIGHT
1010 DATA CHATSWORTH, CALIFORNIA, 91311
```

In the DATA statements there is a comma separating the various elements, unless the DATA statement is at the end of a line. If you have one of the elements out of place or omit a comma, strange things can happen. For example if the READ statement is expecting a numeric variable (such as the street address) and runs into a string (such as the street name) you will get an error message. Think of the DATA statements as a stack of strings and numbers. The first element of the DATA is removed from the stack each time a READ statement is encountered in the program. The next READ statement looks at the element on top of the stack, moving from left to right. Go ahead and SAVE this program and let's put an error in it. (SAVE it first, though, so you will have a correct listing of how READ and DATA statements work.)

LIST the program to make sure you have it in memory and enter the following line:

        85 READ EX$

Now RUN the program and you should get an ?OUT OF DATA ERROR IN 85. The error occurred because you have a READ statement without enough DATA statements (or elements); so, be sure that 1) there are enough elements in your DATA statements to take care of your READ statements, and 2) the variables in your READ statements are compatible with the elements of the DATA statements. (i.e. Your numeric variables read numbers and string variables read strings.) To repair your program, simply type in

        1020 DATA WORD

This will give it something to READ. (Of course you could have DELETEd line 85).

If an element is a DATA statement (and is enclosed in quotation marks), all the characters inside the quotes are considered to be a single string element. For example, make the following changes in your program and RUN it:

145 PRINT EX$
1020 DATA "10 DOWNING ST, LONDON, 45, ENGLAND"

Both numbers and commas were happily accepted by a READ statement
with a string variable since they were all enclosed in quotation marks. Now
remove the quote marks and RUN it again. This time it only printed up to
the first comma, '10 DOWNING ST' but the string variable EX$ had no
problem accepting a numeric character! (However, since it read the '10'
as a string, it cannot be used in a mathematical operation.) Experiment
with different elements in the DATA statements to see what happens. Also,
just for fun, put the DATA statements at different places in the program.
You will quickly find that they can go anywhere and are READ in the order
of placement in the program.

Looping With FOR/NEXT

The FOR/NEXT loop is one of the most useful operations in BASIC programming. It allows the user to instruct the computer to go through a
determined number of steps, at variable increments if desired, and execute them until the total number of steps is completed. Let's look at a
simple example to get started.

```
NEW <RETURN>
10 PRINT "{CLR/HOME}"
20 NA$ = "<YOUR NAME>"
30 FOR I = 1 TO 10 : REM BEGINNING OF LOOP
40 PRINT NA$
50 NEXT I : REM LOOP TERMINAL
60 END
```

Now RUN the program and you will see your name printed 10 times along
the left side of the screen. That's nice, but so what? OK, not too impressive, but we will see how useful this can be in a bit. First let's look at
another simple illustration to show what's happening to "I" as the loop is
being executed.

```
NEW <RETURN>
10 PRINT "{CLR/HOME}"
20 FOR I = 1 TO 10
30 PRINT I
40 NEXT I
```

As we can see when the program is RUN, the value of "I" changes each time the program proceeds through the loop. Think of a loop as a child on a merry-go-round. Each time the merry-go-round completes a revolution, the child gets a gold ring, beginning with one and ending, in our example, with 10.

TRIVIA

As you begin looking at more and more programs, you will see that the variable "I" is used in FOR/NEXT loops a lot. Actually, you can use any variable you want, but the "I" keeps cropping up. Like yourself, I was most curious as to why programmers kept using the letter "I," and after several moments of exhaustive research I found out. The "I" was the "integer" variable in FORTRAN (an early computer language), and it was used in "DO loops" since it was faster. The "I" also can be interpreted to stand for "increment." I told you it was trivia.

Having seen how loops function, let's do something practical with a loop. We'll fix up the CHECKBOOK program we've been playing with.

In our souped up CHECKBOOK program, we are going to use variables in many ways. First, our FOR/NEXT loop will use a variable. We'll stick with tradition and use "I". Second, we will use a variable to indicate the number of loops to be executed. We will use N%, an integer variable. Third, we will use variables for the balance, the amount of the check, and the new balance. This program is going to be a little longer, so be sure to SAVE it to disk every 5 lines or so. For cassette, SAVE it about every 10 lines.

```
NEW <RETURN>
10 PRINT "{CLR/HOME}"
20 CB$ = "CHECK BOOK"
30 PRINT : PRINT : PRINT CB$
40 INPUT "HOW MANY CHECKS? ->" ; N%
50 INPUT "WHAT IS YOUR CURRENT BALANCE? ->" ;BA
60 REM BEGIN LOOP
70 FOR I = 1 TO N%
80 PRINT "YOUR BALANCE IS NOW $";BA
90 PRINT " AMOUNT OF CHECK #";I; "-> ";
100 INPUT CK : REM VARIABLE FOR CHECK
110 BA = BA - CK : REM KEEPS A RUNNING BALANCE
120 NEXT I : REM TOP OF LOOP
```

130 ? "{CLR/HOME}" : REM CLEAR SCREEN WHEN ALL CHECKS ARE ENTERED
140 PRINT : PRINT : PRINT
150 PRINT "YOU NOW HAVE $"; BA ; " IN YOUR ACCOUNT"
160 PRINT : PRINT " THANK YOU AND COME AGAIN "
170 END

Our checkbook program is coming along, making it easier to use, and that is the purpose of computers. Now, let's look at something else with loops.

Nested Loops

With certain applications, it is going to be necessary to have one or more FOR/NEXT loops working inside one another. Let's look at a simple application. Suppose you had two teams with 10 members on each team. You want to make a team roster indicating the team number (#1 or #2) and member number (#1 through #10). Using a nested loop, we can do this in the following program:

```
NEW <RETURN>
10 PRINT "{CLR/HOME}"
20 FOR T = 1 TO 2 : REM T FOR TEAM #
30 FOR M = 1 TO 10 : REM M FOR MEMBER #
40 PRINT "TEAM #" ; T ; "PLAYER #"; M
50 NEXT M
60 NEXT T
70 END
```

In using nested loops, it is important to keep the loops straight. The inner-most loop (the "M loop" in our example) must not have any other FOR or NEXT statement inside of it. Think of nested loops as a series of fish eating one another, the largest fish's mouth encompassing the next largest and so forth on down to the smallest fish.

Look at the following structure of nested loops:

```
FOR A = 1 TO N
   FOR B = 1 TO N
      FOR C = 1 TO N
         FOR D = 1 TO N
         NEXT D
      NEXT C
   NEXT B
NEXT A
```

Note how each loop begins (a FOR statement is executed) and is termi-nated (encounters a NEXT statement) in a "nested" sequence. If you have ever stacked a set of different sized cooking bowls, each one fits inside the other; that is because the outer edge of one is larger than the next one. Likewise, in nested loops, the "edge" of each loop is "larger" than the one inside it and "smaller" than the one it is inside.

Stepping Forward and Backwards

Loops can go one step at a time, as we have been using, or they can step at different increments. For example, the following program "steps" by 10.

```
NEW <RETURN>
10 PRINT "{CLR/HOME}"
20 FOR I = 10 TO 100 STEP 10
30 PRINT I
40 NEXT I
```

This allows you to increment your count by whatever you want. You can even use variables or anything else that has a numeric value. For example

```
NEW <RETURN>
10 PRINT "{CLR/HOME}"
20 K = 5 : N = 25
30 FOR I = K TO N STEP K
40 PRINT I
50 NEXT
```

Go ahead and RUN the program. But WAIT!!, you say. In line 50 you detect a BUG, a typo and big mistake. After the word NEXT, there should be an "I" but there is none, right? Well, actually, in COMMODORE-64 BASIC you really do not need it, and you can save a little memory if you use NEXT statements without the variable name. Even in nested loops, as long as you put in enough NEXT statements, it is possible to run your program without variable names after NEXT statements. However, it is good programming practice to use variable names after NEXT statements, especially in nested loops so that you can keep everything straight.

It is also possible to go backwards. Try this program:

```
NEW <RETURN>
10 FOR I = 4 TO 1 STEP -1
20 PRINT "FINISHING POSITION IN RACE =";I
30 NEXT I
```

As we get into more and more sophisticated (and useful) programs, we will begin to see how all of these different features of COMMODORE-64 BASIC are very useful. Often you may not see the practicality of a command initially, but when you need it later on, you will wonder how you could program without it!

Counters

Often you will want to count the number of times a loop is executed and keep a record of it in your program for later use. For example, if you run a program that loops with a STEP of 3, you may not know exactly how many times the loop will execute. To find out, programmers use "counters," variables that are incremented, usually by $+1$, each time a loop is executed. The following program illustrates the use of a counter:

```
NEW <RETURN>
10 PRINT "{CLR/HOME}
20 FOR I = 3 TO 99 STEP 3
30 PRINT I
40 N = N + 1 : REM THIS IS THE COUNTER
50 NEXT I
60 PRINT : PRINT "YOUR LOOP EXECUTED "; N ; " TIMES."
```

The first time the loop was entered, the value of "N" was 0; when the program got to line 40, the value of 1 was added to N to make it 1 (i.e. $0 + 1 = 1$). The second time through the loop, the value of N began at 1, then 1 was added. At the top of the loop, line 50, the value of N was 2. This went on until the program exited the loop. When all of the looping was finished, presto!, your N told you how many times the loop was executed. Of course, counters are not restricted to counting loops, and they can be incremented by any value, including other variables, you need. For example, change line 40 to read:

```
40 N = N + (I * 2)
```

RUN your program again and your "counter total" will be a good deal higher.

Summary

This chapter has begun to show you the power of your computer, and we have really began programming. One of the most important concepts we have covered is that of the "variable." The significant feature of variables is that they "vary" (change depending on what your program does). This is true not only with numeric variables, but also with string variables. The various input commands show how we enter values or strings into variables depending on what we want the computer to compute for us. Finally, we have learned how to loop. This allows us, with a minimal amount of effort, to tell the computer to go through a process several times with a single set of instructions. With loops we can set the parameters of an operation at any increment we want, and then sit back and let our COMMODORE-64's go to work for us.

However, we have only just begun programming! In the next chapter we will begin getting into more commands and operations that allow us to delve deeper into the COMMODORE-64's capabilities and make our programming jobs easier. The more commands we know, the less work it is to write a program.

CHAPTER 4

Branching Out

Introduction

In this chapter we will begin exploring new programming constructs which will geometrically increase your programming ability. We will be examining some more sophisticated techniques, but by taking each a step at a time, you will begin using them with ease. Later, when you are developing your own programs, be bold and try out new commands. One problem common to new programmers is a tendency to stick with the simple commands they have learned to get a job done. After all, why use "complicated" commands to do what simpler ones can do? Well, the answer to that has to do with simplicity. If one "complicated" command can do the work of 10 "simple" commands, which one is actually simpler? As you get into more and more sophisticated programming applications, your programs can become longer and subject to more bugs. The more commands you have to sift through, the more difficult it is to find the bugs; therefore, while it is perfectly OK to write a long program using a lot of simple commands while you're learning, begin thinking about short-cuts through the use of the more advanced commands.

Related to this issue of maximizing your knowledge of different commands is that of letting the computer perform the computing. This may sound strange at first, but often novices will figure everything out for the computer and use it as a glorified calculator. In the last chapter you may remember that we set up a counter to count the times a loop was executed when we used a STEP 3 loop. We could have figured out how many loops were executed instead of letting the computer do it with the counter, but that would have defeated the purpose of programming! So, as you learn new commands, see how they can be used to perform the calculations you had to work out yourself.

Branching

So far all of our programs have gone straight from the top to the bottom with the exception of loops. However, if our COMMODORE-64 is to do some real decision making, we must have some way of giving it options. When a program leaves a straight path, it is referred to as either "looping" or "branching." We already know the purpose of a loop, but what is a branch? Well, using the IF/THEN and GOTO commands, we will see. (In fact, with the GET statement in the last chapter, we sneaked these commands in.) Consider the following program: (NOTE: By now you should know enough to clear memory with a NEW command, so I won't keep on insulting your intelligence by putting one at the beginning of each program.)

```
10 PRINT "{CLR/HOME}"
20 PRINT "CHOOSE ONE OF THE FOLLOWING BY NUMBER:"
30 PRINT
40 PRINT "1. BANANAS"
50 PRINT "2. ORANGES"
60 PRINT "3. PEACHES"
70 PRINT "4. WATERMELONS"
80 PRINT
90 INPUT "WHICH? "; X
100 PRINT "{CLR/HOME}"
110 IF X = 1 THEN GOTO 200
120 IF X = 2 THEN GOTO 300
130 IF X = 3 THEN GOTO 400
140 IF X = 4 THEN GOTO 500
150 GOTO 10 : REM THIS IS A 'TRAP' TO MAKE SURE THE
USER CHOOSES 1, 2, 3, OR 4
200 PRINT "BANANAS" : END
300 PRINT "ORANGES" : END
400 PRINT "PEACHES" : END
500 PRINT "WATERMELONS" : END
```

As you can see, your computer "branched" to the appropriate place, did what it was told and ENDed. Not very inspiring I admit, but it is a clear example. Now, let's try something a little more practical for your kids to play with in their math homework.

```
10 PRINT "{CLR/HOME}"
20 AG$ = " ADDITION GAME ": PRINT AG$
30 PRINT : PRINT
40 INPUT "ENTER FIRST NUMBER -->" ; A
50 PRINT
60 INPUT "ENTER SECOND NUMBER-->" ; B
70 PRINT
80 PRINT "WHAT IS "; A ; "+" ; B ; : INPUT C
90 IF C = A + B THEN GOTO 200
100 PRINT : PRINT "THAT'S NOT QUITE IT. TRY AGAIN." : PRINT
110 GOTO 80
200 PRINT " THAT'S RIGHT! VERY GOOD "
210 PRINT
220 PRINT "WOULD YOU LIKE TO DO MORE? (Y/N): ";
230 GET AN$ : IF AN$ = "" THEN GOTO 230
240 IF AN$ = "Y" THEN PRINT"{CLR/HOME}" : GOTO 30
250 PRINT"{CLR/HOME}" : PRINT : PRINT : PRINT
260 PRINT "HOPE TO SEE YOU AGAIN SOON" : END
```

As you can see, the more commands we learn, the more fun we can have. Just for fun, change the program so that it will handle multiplication, division, and subtraction.

Let's look carefully at our program to learn something about IF/THEN statements. First, note in line 240, the branch is to clear the screen (PRINT"{CLR/HOME}") if AN$ = "Y". If any other response is encountered it ends the program. You may ask why the program did not branch to line 30 regardless of the response since the "GOTO 30" command is after a colon, making it a new line. Good point. The reason for that is after an IF statement, when the response or condition is null, the program immediately drops to the next LINE NUMBER. That is, any statements after a colon in a line beginning with an IF statement will only be executed if the condition of the IF statement is met. Secondly, the condition of AN$ is queried as being a "Y" and not simply a Y without quotes. Since the user INPUTs a Y and not a "Y", we assume that the program will accept a Y, but remember AN$ is a "string" and not a numeric variable. Therefore in the setting of the conditional, we must remember what kind of variable we are using. On the other hand, if we used a numeric variable, such as AN or AN%, we could have entered a line such as,

        IF AN = 1 THEN....

Relationals

So far we have only used " = " to determine whether or not our program should branch. However, there are other states, referred to as "relationals," that we can also query. The following is a complete list of the relationals we can employ:

SYMBOL	MEANING
=	Equal to
<	Less than
>	Greater than
<>	Not equal to
>=	Greater than or equal to
<=	Less than or equal to

Now let's play with some of these, and then we'll examine them for their full power. Here are some quickie programs:

```
10 PRINT "{CLR/HOME}"
20 INPUT "NUMBER 1-->";A
30 INPUT "NUMBER 2-->";B
40 IF A > B THEN GOTO 100
50 IF A < B THEN GOTO 200
60 IF A = B THEN GOTO 300
100 PRINT "NUMBER 1 IS GREATER THAN NUMBER 2" : END
200 PRINT "NUMBER 1 IS LESS THAN NUMBER 2" : END
300 PRINT "NUMBER 1 IS EQUAL TO NUMBER 2"

10 PRINT "{CLR/HOME}"
20 INPUT "DO YOU WANT TO CONTINUE? (Y/N)"; AN$
30 IF AN$ <> "Y" THEN END
40 GOTO 10
```

```
10 PRINT "{CLR/HOME}"
20 INPUT "HOW OLD ARE YOU? "; AG%
30 IF AG% > = 21 THEN GOTO 100
40 PRINT"{CLR/HOME}" : PRINT : PRINT "SORRY, YOU'VE
GOT TO BE 21 OR OLDER TO COME IN HERE!" : END
100 PRINT"{CLR/HOME}" : PRINT : PRINT "WHAT WOULD
YOU LIKE TO DRINK?"
```

OK, you have the idea how relationals can be used with IF/THEN commands; note they work with strings as well as numeric variables. However, there is another way to use relationals. Try the following from the Immediate mode:

```
A = 10 : B = 20 : PRINT A = B
```

Your computer responded with a 0, right? This is a logical operation. If a condition is false, your COMMODORE-64 responds with a 0; but if it is true, it responds with a -1. Now try the following little program.

```
10 PRINT "{CLR/HOME}"
20 A = 10
30 B = 20
40 C = A > B
50 PRINT C
```

When you RUN the program, you again get a 0. This is because the variable C was defined as A being greater than B. Since A was less than B the variable C was 0 or "false." Now, let's take it a step further:

```
10 PRINT "{CLR/HOME}"
20 A = 10
30 B = 20
40 C = A > B
50 IF C = 0 THEN PRINT "A IS LESS THAN B" : END
60 IF C = -1 THEN PRINT "A IS GREATER THAN B"
```

Later, we will see further applications of these logical operations of the COMMODORE-64. For now, though, it is important to understand that a true condition is represented by a "-1" and a false condition by a "0".

AND/OR/NOT

Sometimes we need to set up more than a single relational. Suppose, for example, that you are organizing your finances into 3 categories of expenses: (1) Under $10, (2) between $10 and $100, and 3) over $100. With our relationals it would be simple to compare input under $10 and over $100.

But what if we wanted to do something in between. In this case we might have some difficulty without added commands. The AND, OR and NOT statements allow us to set ranges with our relationals.

AND	If all conditions are met then true
OR	If one condition is met then true
NOT	If condition is not met then true.

For example:

```
10 PRINT "{CLR/HOME}"
20 INPUT "ENTER AMOUNT -->$"; A
30 IF A <= 10 THEN 100
40 IF A <= 100 THEN 200
50 IF A > 100 THEN 300
100 PRINT " PETTY CASH " : GOTO 400
200 PRINT " GENERAL EXPENSES " :GOTO 400
300 PRINT " BIG BUCKS "
400 PRINT " DO YOU WISH TO CONTINUE? "
410 GET AN$ : IF AN$ = "" THEN 410
420 IF AN$ < > "Y" AND AN$ < > "N" THEN PRINT "ANSWER
'Y' OR 'N' PLEASE " : GOTO 400
430 IF AN$ = "Y" THEN 10
440 PRINT"{CLR/HOME}" : PRINT "GOODBYE"
```

In line 40 we set the conditional branch to be BOTH greater than 10 and equal to or less than 100. The variable "A" had to meet both conditions to branch. Similarly, in line 420, using the AND statement again, we made sure that the response had to be either "Y" or "N".

If you are very perceptive, you may have asked yourself about some fishy format in the program. There are conditional IF/THEN lines that simply say THEN 100 and stuff like that. What's going on? Shouldn't there be a GOTO statement there? Again, we have slipped in another feature of COMMODORE-64 BASIC. When using IF/THEN statements, it is possible to drop the GOTO on a branch and simply put in the line number. However, note that we have used GOTO statements elsewhere in the program where no conditional is used within the same line or within a single set of colons. Until you become more familiar with programming you might want to keep your GOTO statements after IF/THEN statements, but they are not required.

You may have had another question which involves the AND statement in line 420. In normal English if we say something is not "Y" or "N" we mean that it must be one or the other. However, in programming, if we use OR, we are telling the program to branch if either condition is met. Thus, if we wrote line 420 as,

```
420 IF AN$ < > "Y" OR AN$ < > "N" THEN PRINT "ANSWER
'Y' OR 'N' PLEASE " : GOTO 400
```

the program would have branched if AN$ was not equal to EITHER "Y" or "N". Thus, for example, if we responded with a "Y", that "Y" would have NOT been equal to "N" and so the program would have branched to "ANSWER 'Y' OR 'N' PLEASE" - not what we intended. To check this, change the AND to an OR in line 420 and RUN the program.

Now, let's use the OR and NOT statements in a program:

```
10 PRINT "{CLR/HOME}"
20 READ A
30 READ B
40 READ C
50 DATA 10,20,30
60 IF A + B = C OR A < B OR A − B = C THEN 100
70 END
100 PRINT"{CLR/HOME}" : PRINT "ONE OF 'EM MUST BE
TRUE"
```

Looking at line 60 we can see that A − B does not equal C; however, A + B does equal C and A is less than B. Using the OR statement, only one statement has to be true to branch. Now, let's try the following program:

```
10 PRINT "{CLR/HOME}"
20 READ A : READ B : READ C
30 DATA 10,20,30
40 Z = A − B = C
50 IF NOT Z THEN 100
60 END
100 PRINT " THAT'S RIGHT! A - B = C IS NOT RIGHT! - DID
I SAY THAT RIGHT?"
```

As can be seen from the example, it is possible to use the "negation" of a formula to calculate a branch condition. In most cases, you will use < > (not equal) or the positive case, but at other times it will be simpler to employ NOT.

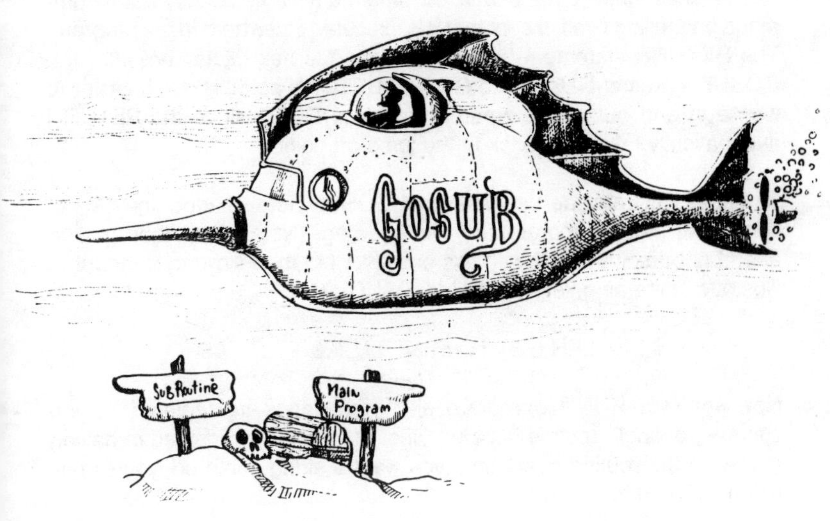

Subroutines

Often in programming there is some operation you will want your computer to perform at several different places in the program. Now, you can repeat the instructions again and again or use GOTO's all over the place to return to your original spot after branching to the operation. On the other hand, you can set up "subroutines" and jump to them using GOSUB and get back to your starting point using the RETURN command. Up to a point the GOSUB command works pretty much like the GOTO command since it sends your program bouncing off to a line out of sequence. Also, the RETURN command is something like GOTO since it also sends your program to an out-of-sequence line. However, the GOSUB/RETURN pair is unique in what it does. Let's take a look at a simple example to see how it works:

```
10 PRINT "{CLR/HOME}"
20 A$ = "HELLO" : GOSUB 100
30 A$ = "HOW ARE YOU TODAY?" : GOSUB 100
40 A$ = "I'M FINE" : GOSUB 100
50 END
100 PRINT A$
110 RETURN
```

Our example shows that a GOSUB statement works exactly like a command on the line itself except that it is executed elsewhere in the program. The RETURN statement brings it back to the next statement after the GOSUB statement. Using the GOSUB/RETURN pair it is much easier to weave in and out of a program than using GOTO since the RETURN automatically takes you back to the jump-off point.

To better illustrate the usefulness of GOSUB, let's change line 100 to something more elaborate. Try the following. (Note: We will be getting ahead of ourselves a bit with this example, but the following is meant to illustrate something very useful in GOSUB's.)

```
100 L = LEN (A$)/2 : PRINT TAB(20 − L ) ; A$
```

Now when you RUN the program, all of your strings are centered. As you can see, a single routine handled all of the centering. Instead of having to rewrite the routine every time you want a string centered, you simply use a GOSUB to line 100.

NEATNESS COUNTS

We really have not discussed the structure of programs too much up to this point. In part, this is because it was not really necessary. However, as our instruction set grows, so too does the possibility for errors. By now, if you haven't made an error, you haven't been keying in these programs! You can to minimize errors, especially using GOSUB's, by organizing them into coherent "blocks." Basically, a "block" is a subroutine within a range of lines. For example, you might block your subroutines by 100's or 1000's, depending on how long the subroutines are. Thus, you might have subroutines beginning at lines 500, 600 and 700. It doesn't matter if the subroutine is 1 line or 10 lines, as long as it is confined to the block. It is easier to debug, easier for others and you to understand what is happening in the program, and in general a good programming practice.

Computed GOTO and GOSUB

Now we're going to get a little fancier, but in the long run, it will result in clearer and simpler programming. As we have seen, we can GOTO or GOSUB on a "conditional" (e.g. IF A = 1 THEN GOTO 200). The easier way to make a conditional jump is to use "computed" branches using the ON statement. For example,

```
10 PRINT "{CLR/HOME}"
20 INPUT "ENTER A NUMBER FROM 1 TO 5 " ; A
30 IF A < 1 OR A > 5 THEN 20 : REM TRAP
40 ON A GOSUB 100,200,300,400,500 : REM COMPUTED
GOSUB
50 PRINT "DO YOU WISH TO CONTINUE? (Y/N)" ;
60 GET AN$ : IF AN$ = "" THEN 60
70 IF AN$ < > "Y" THEN END
80 GOTO 10
100 PRINT "ONE" : PRINT : RETURN
200 PRINT "TWO" : PRINT : RETURN
300 PRINT "THREE" : PRINT : RETURN
400 PRINT "FOUR" : PRINT : RETURN
500 PRINT "FIVE" : PRINT : RETURN
```

To format a computed GOSUB/GOTO enter a variable following the ON command. The program will then jump the number of "commas" to the appropriate line number. If a 1 is entered, it takes the first line number, a 2, the second, and so forth. It's a lot easier than entering, " IF A = 1 THEN GOSUB 100 : IF A = 2 THEN GOSUB 200 : etc. " However, it is necessary to use relatively small numbers in the "ON" variable since there is a limited number of subroutines. If your program is computing larger numbers, just convert the larger numbers into smaller ones by changing the variables. For example:

```
10 PRINT "{CLR/HOME}"
20 INPUT "ENTER ANY NUMBER--> "; A
30 IF A < 100 THEN B = 1
40 IF A >= 100 AND A < 200 THEN B = 2
50 IF A >= 200 THEN B = 3
60 ON B GOSUB 100, 200, 300 : REM COMPUTED GOSUB
ON 'B' VARIABLE
70 PRINT "DO YOU WISH TO CONTINUE?(Y/N)";
80 GET AN$ : IF AN$ = "" THEN 80
90 IF AN$ < > "Y" THEN END
95 GOTO 10
100 PRINT "LESS THAN 100" : RETURN
200 PRINT "MORE THAN 100 BUT LESS THAN 200 " : RETURN
300 PRINT "MORE THAN 200" : RETURN
```

RUN the program and enter any number you want. Since the program is branching on the variable B and not on A (the INPUT variable), you will not get an error since the greatest value of B can only be 3.

Now let's get back to relationals and see how they can be used with computed GOSUBS. Remember, in using relationals, the only numbers we get are 0's and 1's for false and true respectively. However, we can use these 0's and 1's just like regular numbers. Try the following:

```
10 PRINT "{CLR/HOME}"
20 X = 1 : Y = 2 : Z = 3
30 A = X < Z
40 B = Y > Z
50 C = Z > X
60 PRINT "A + A =" ; A + A
70 PRINT : PRINT "A + B =" ; A + B
80 PRINT : PRINT "A + B + C =" ; A + B + C
90 END
```

Now before you RUN the program, see if you can determine what will be printed by lines 60, 70 and 80. Once you have made a determination, RUN the program and see what happens. Go ahead and do it. How'd you do? Let's go over it step by step.

1. Since X is less than Z, A will be "true" with a value of one (-1). Therefore A + A ($-1 + -1$) will equal -2.

2. Since Y is not less than Z , (Y = 2 and Z = 3, remember) B will be "false" with a value of 0. Therefore, A + B ($-1 + 0$) will total -1.

3. Since Z is greater than X, C will be "true" with a value of -1. Therefore A + B + C ($-1 + 0 + -1$) will equal -2.

If you got it right, congratulations! If not, go over it again. Remember, very simple things are happening, so don't look for a complicated explanation!

Now that we see how we can get numbers by manipulating relationals, let's use them in computed GOSUB's. The following program shows how:

```
10 PRINT "{CLR/HOME}"
20 INPUT "HOW BIG WAS THE HOME CROWD?"; HC
30 R = 1 + (HC >= 500) + (HC >= 1000)
40 IF R = 0 THEN R = 2
50 IF R = -1 THEN R = 3
60 ON R GOSUB 100,200,300
70 PRINT : INPUT "DO YOU WISH TO CONTINUE? (Y/N) "; AN$
80 IF AN$ < > "Y" THEN END
```

90 GOTO 10
100 PRINT "{CLR/HOME}" : PRINT "THE HOME CROWD WAS
NOT VERY BIG - LESS THAN 500" : RETURN
200 PRINT "{CLR/HOME}" : PRINT "THE HOME CROWD WAS
A PRETTY GOOD SIZE - BETWEEN 500 AND 1000." : RETURN
300 PRINT "{CLR/HOME}" : PRINT "THE HOME CROWD WAS
VERY BIG - 1000 OR OVER! " : RETURN

This program is hinged on line 30's formula or algorithm. Let's see how it works:

1. There are 3 conditions:

   a. HC is less than 500
   b. HC is between 500 and 1000
   c. HC is greater than 1000

2. If the first condition exists, both HC >= 500 and HC >= 1000 would be false. Thus $1 + 0 + 0 = 1$. Therefore R = 1.

3. If HC is >= 500 but less than 1000 then HC >= 500 would be true but HC >= 1000 would be false. Thus we would have $1 + (-1) + 0 = 0$. Convert the value of R to 2.

4. Finally if HC is both >= 500 and >=1000 then our formula would result in $1 + (-1) + (-1) = -1$. Convert the value of R to 3.

REST AREA

At this point let's take a little rest and reflection. In programming, there is no such thing as THE RIGHT WAY and THE WRONG WAY. Certain programs are more efficient, faster or take less code and memory than others, but the computer makes no moral judgments. If a program does what you want it to do, no matter how slowly it does it or how long it took you to write it, it is "right." In the above example we used an algorithm with relationals to do something we could have done with more code. Don't expect to use such formulas right off the bat unless you have a strong background in math. If you're not used to using algorithms, don't expect to understand their full potential right away. The one we used is relatively simple. You will find far more elaborate ones as you begin looking at more programs. The main point is to keep plugging ahead. With practice you will learn all kinds of little shortcuts and formulas. If you get stuck along the way, just keep on going. Remember, as long as you can get your program running the way you want it to, you're doing the "right" thing.

Before we leave our discussion of computed GOTO's and GOSUB's with relationals, let's take a look at how relationals handle strings. Try the following:

A$ = "A" : B$ = "B" : PRINT B$ > A$ <RETURN>

Surprised? In addition to comparing numeric variables, relationals can compare alphabetic string variables with "A" being the lowest and "Z" the highest. So if we ask is B$ greater than A$, we get a " − 1" (true) since B$ was a B and A$ was an A. Now you might be wondering what on earth you could possibly want to do with this knowledge. Well, in sorting strings (like putting names in alphabetical order) such an operation is crucial. Later on we will show you a routine for sorting strings, but for now let's make a simple string sorter for sorting two strings.

```
10 PRINT "{CLR/HOME}"
20 INPUT "WORD #1 --> " ; A$
30 INPUT "WORD #2 --> " ; B$
40 PRINT : PRINT : PRINT
50 IF A$ < B$ THEN PRINT A$ : PRINT B$
60 IF A$ > B$ THEN PRINT B$ : PRINT A$
```

Just what you needed! A program which will put two words in alphabetical order!

Arrays

The best way to think about arrays is as a kind of variable. As we have seen, we can name variables A, D$, KK%, X1 and so forth. An array uses a single name with a number to differentiate different variables. Consider the following two lists, one using regular string variables and the other using a string array:

STRING VARIABLE	STRING ARRAY
P$ = "PIG"	AM$(1) = "PIG"
C$ = "CHICKEN"	AM$(2) = "CHICKEN"
D$ = "DOG"	AM$(3) = "DOG"
H$ = "HORSE"	AM$(4) = "HORSE"

Now if we PRINT H$ we'd get HORSE and if we PRINT AM$(4) we'd also get HORSE. Likewise, we could use arrays for numeric variables such as:

A(1) = 1
A(2) = 2
A(3) = 3
A(4) = 4 etc.

Again you may well ask, "So what? Why not just use regular numeric or string variables instead of arrays?" Well, for one thing, using arrays makes it easier to keep track of what you're doing in a program. For another, using arrays saves a lot of time. Consider the following program for INPUTing a list of 10 names using a string array.

```
10 PRINT "{CLR/HOME}"
20 FOR I = 1 TO 10
30 PRINT "NAME #"; I ; : INPUT NA$(I)
40 NEXT I
50 FOR I = 1 TO 10 : PRINT NA$(I)
60 NEXT I
```

Now, write a program which does the same thing using non-array variables. It would take a lot more code to do so, but go ahead and try it. Use the variables N0$ through N9$ for the names just to see what it would take.

If you re-wrote the program, you saw how much time using arrays saved. Before going on, let's take a closer look at how the program worked with the FOR/NEXT loop and array variable:

1. The FOR/NEXT loop generated the numbers sequentially so that the array would be the following:

```
FOR I = 1 TO 10
NA$(1) <--First time through loop
NA$(2) <--Second time through loop
NA$(3) <--Third time through loop
NA$(4) etc.
NA$(5)
NA$(6)
NA$(7)
NA$(8)
NA$(9)
NA$(10)
NEXT I
```

2. Each string INPUT by the user was stored in a sequentially numbered array variable.

3. Output, using the PRINT statement, was generated by the FOR/NEXT loop sequentially supplying numbers to be entered into array variables.

Now to get used to the idea that an array variable is a variable, enter the following:

```
A(10) = 432 : PRINT A(10) <RETURN>
XYZ(9) = 2.432 : PRINT XYZ(9) <RETURN>
R2D2$(1) = "BEEP!" + CHR$(7) : PRINT R2D2$(1) <RETURN>
J%(5) = 321 : PRINT J%(5) <RETURN>
```

OK, maybe it didn't take all that to convince you that an array is a variable with a number in parentheses after it, but it's easy to forget and think of arrays as something more exotic than they are.

THE DIMension of an ARRAY

If you've been very observant, you may have noticed we haven't gone over the number 10 in our array examples. The reason behind that is because once our array is larger than 10 we have to use the DIM (dimension) statement to reserve space for our array. (Actually 11 array elements are automatically dimensioned - 0 to 10.) The following is an example of the format for DIMensioning an array.

```
10 PRINT "{CLR/HOME}"
20 DIM AB(150) : REM DIMENSION OF ARRAY VARIABLE 'AB'
30 FOR I = 1 TO 150
40 AB(I) = I
50 NEXT I
60 FOR I = 1 TO 150
70 PRINT AB(I),
80 NEXT I
```

RUN the program as it is written. It should work fine. Now delete line 20 by simply entering 20. (Remember how we learned to delete single line numbers by entering that number?) Now RUN the program and you will get an error for not DIMing the ARRAY. (?BAD SUBSCRIPT ERROR IN 40 - that's because there was no DIM statement in Line 20). So, whenever your arrays are going to have more than 11 values from 0 to10, be sure to DIM them.

BETTER SAFE THAN SORRY DEPT.

Many programmers always DIM arrays, regardless of the number in the array. It is perfectly all right to do so, and statements such as DIM X$(3) or DIM N% (5) are valid. Often, when copying programs from books or magazines, you may run across these lower level DIM statements not because they are necessary, but rather because the programmer thinks it's a good idea to DIM all arrays as part of programming style and clarity.

Multi-dimensional Arrays

So far, we have examined only single dimension arrays. However, it is possible to have arrays with two or more dimensions. Let's begin with two-dimensional arrays, and examine how to use arrays with more than a single dimension.

The best way to think of a 2-dimensional array is as a matrix. For example if our array ranged from 1 to 3 on two dimensions the entire set would include: A(1,1) A(1,2) A(1,3) A(2,1) A(2,2) A(2,3) A(3,1) A(3,2) and A(3,3). By laying it out on a matrix, we can think of the first number as a row and the second as a column. This makes it much clearer:

	COLUMN #1	COLUMN #2	COLUMN #3
ROW #1	A(1,1)	A(1,2)	A(1,3)
ROW #2	A(2,1)	A(2,2)	A(2,3)
ROW #3	A(3,1)	A(3,2)	A(3,3)

Again, it is important to remember that each element in the array is simply a type of variable. To drum that into your head do the following:

```
XV$(3,1) = "I'M A VARIABLE" : PRINT XV$(3,1) <RETURN>
JK%(2,2) = 21 : PRINT JK% (2,2) <RETURN>
MM (1,1) = 3.212 : PRINT MM(1,1) <RETURN>
```

OK, so you were reminded a bit much; but in order to use arrays to their fullest advantage in programs, they must be envisioned as an orderly set of variables and not something else. Now let's use a 2-dimension array in a program. Our program will be to line up people in a 12 member marching band.

```
10 PRINT "{CLR/HOME}"
20 DIM BA$(4,4) : REM MAKE 3 'ROWS' AND 3 'COLUMNS'
30 FOR I = 1 TO 4 : REM ROWS
40 FOR J = 1 TO 4 : REM COLUMNS
50 READ BA$(I,J)
60 NEXT J
70 NEXT I
90 DATA RALPH, PAT, DARLENE, FRANK, HORACE, DAVID,
KARL, ERIC
95 DATA MARY, TOM, SUE, PETE, JACK, NANCY, BETTY, BILL
100 REM OUTPUT BLOCK
110 FOR I = 1 TO 4 : REM ROWS
120 FOR J = 1 TO 4 : REM COLUMNS
130 PRINT BA$(I,J) , : REM COMMA WILL FORMAT OUTPUT
4 ACROSS
140 NEXT J
150 NEXT I
```

When you RUN this program, all of your band members will be lined up.
However, you could have done the same thing with a single dimension
array since all that "lines them up" is the use of the comma to format the
PRINT statement in line 130. So what's the big deal about a 2-dimension
array? Well, to see, let's add some lines to our program:

```
160 PRINT : PRINT "HIT ANY KEY TO CONTINUE ";
170 GET AN$:IF AN$ = "" THEN 170
180 PRINT "{CLR/HOME}" : PRINT "WHAT ROW & COLUMN
WOULD YOU LIKE TO SEE? "
190 INPUT "ROW #-> ";R
200 INPUT "COL #-> ";C
210 PRINT : PRINT BA$(R,C); " IS IN ROW "; R; " COLUMN ";
C
220 PRINT : PRINT "MORE?(Y/N) ";
230 GET M$ : IF M$ = "" THEN 230
240 IF M$ = "Y" THEN 180
```

Now you can locate the value or contents of a specific array on two
dimensions. In our example if you know the row number and column
number, you can find the band member in that position. The use of 2-
dimensional arrays in problems dealing with matrixes is an important
addition to your programming commands.

It is also possible to have several more dimensions in an array variable.
As you add more and more dimensions, you have to be careful not to
confuse the different aspects of a single array. Sometimes, when a multi-
dimensional array becomes difficult to manage (or use), it is better to

break it down into several 1- or 2-dimensional arrays. But just for fun, let's see what we might want to do with a 3 dimensional array with the following program : (By the way, this problem is based on an actual application!)

```
10 PRINT "{CLR/HOME}"
20 PRINT "WINECELLAR ORGANIZER "
30 PRINT : PRINT "HOW MANY RACKS,ROWS, COLUMNS?"
35 INPUT "(ENTER EACH SEPARATED BY A COMMA)";RK,R,C
40 DIM WI$(RK,R,C)
50 INPUT "HOW MANY BOTTLES TO STORE? ";N%
60 PRINT : FOR I = 1 TO N%
70 INPUT "RACK #-> ";RA
80 INPUT "ROW #-> ";RO
90 INPUT "COL #-> ";CO
100 INPUT "NAME OF WINE : ";WN$
110 WI$(RA,RO,CO) = WN$
120 NEXT I
200 REM ROUTINE FOR CHECKING CONTENTS OF WINE
CELLAR
210 PRINT "{CLR/HOME}" : INPUT "WHICH RACK # WOULD
YOU LIKE TO CHECK? ";RR
220 FOR I = 1 TO R
230 FOR J = 1 TO C
240 IF WI$(RR,I,J) = "" THEN WI$(RR,I,J) = "EMPTY"
250 PRINT "RACK #";RR;" ROW #";I;" COLUMN #";J;" CON-
TAINS ";WI$(RR,I,J)
260 NEXT J
270 NEXT I
280 END
```

Now that was a pretty long program, but go over it carefully to make sure you understand what it is doing. Again, let me remind you that the 3-dimensional array is just a variable with a lot of numbers in parentheses. Also, note on line 35 how we INPUT several values with a single INPUT statement. We used the format

```
INPUT A, B, C
```

and as long as the operator (program user) is told to enter the appropriate number of responses and separate each with a comma, every thing will work fine. Also, it would be a good idea to save this program on a disk as an example of a multi-dimensional array.

Summary

We covered a good deal in this chapter. If you understood everything, excellent! If you did not, don't worry; with practice, it will all become very clear. Whatever your understanding of the material, though, experiment with all the statements. Be BOLD and daring with your computer's commands. As long as you have a disk or cassette on which you can practice your skills, at worst you will erase a few programs!

We learned that your COMMODORE-64 computer can compute! Using the IF/THEN commands and relationals we can give the computer the power of "decision making." Using subroutines it is possible to branch at decision points to anywhere we want in our program. Computed GOTOs and GOSUBs allow the execution to move appropriately with a minimal amount of programming.

Finally, we examined array variables. Arrays allow us to enter values into sequentially arranged variables (or elements). Using FOR/NEXT loops it is possible to quickly program multiple variables up to the limits of our DIMensions. Not only do arrays assist us in keeping variables orderly, they save a good deal of work as well.

In the next chapter, we will begin working with commands which help arrange everything for us. As our programs become more and more sophisticated, we will need to keep better track of what we're doing. We can create clear useful programs by organizing our programs into small, manageable chunks.

CHAPTER 5

Organizing the Parts

Introduction

Unless we organize as we accumulate more and more information, work, or just about anything else, things get confusing. Good organization allows us to do more and to handle more complex and larger problems. These principles hold with programming. As we learn more commands, we can do more things; but the more we do, the more likely we are to get tangled up and lost.

Formatting output is one of the areas which is likely to be the first to suffer from "overflow." Variables get mixed up, arrays are misnumbered and the screen is a mess. In order to handle this kind of problem, we will deal extensively with text and string formatting. Not only will we be able to put things where we want them, but we will do it with style!

The second major area of disorganization is I/O (INPUT/OUTPUT). Some of the problem has to do with formatting, but even more elementary is the problem of organizing the input and output so that data is properly analyzed. Data has to be connected to the proper variables and be subject to the correct computations. Thus, in addition to examining string formatting, we will also look at organizing data manipulation.

Formatting Text

In Chapter 1 we said that the COMMODORE-64 keyboard works like a typewriter in many ways. One feature of a typewriter is its ability to set "tabs" so that the user can automatically place text a given number of spaces from the left margin. With your COMMODORE-64, you can TAB and SPC. Let's look at what each of these means:

COMMAND	MEANING
TAB (N)	Used within PRINT statement to place next character N spaces from left margin
SPC (N)	Used within PRINT statement, creates specified number of spaces. (SPC starts printing non-space 1 space after N).
{HOME}	Places cursor in upper left hand corner of screen. Use the CLR/HOME key *without* pressing SHIFT key.

Now, to better see how these commands format text output, let's USE THEM!

```
10 PRINT "{CLR/HOME}" : PRINT : PRINT
20 PRINT TAB (20);"TAB TO HERE"
30 PRINT SPC(20);"SPC TO HERE"
40 PRINT "{HOME}";"UP HERE!" : REM PRESS THE CLR/HOME
KEY WITHOUT THE SHIFT KEY - YOU'LL GET AN INVERSE
"S"
50 FOR I = 1 TO 20 : PRINT : NEXT : PRINT "DOWN HERE"
```

When you RUN this program, note that when you used the {HOME} command, it did not clear the screen. Rather, it placed the cursor at the top of the screen, leaving what was printed in lines 20 and 30 on the screen. Also, we were able to produce a vertical tab by using an empty PRINT statement in line 50 to take the text down to vertical position 20 on the screen. Again, the other text on the screen was not erased. Now let's have a little fun with our commands. Here's a little program which will give you an idea of how to place text within your program.

```
10 PRINT "{CLR/HOME}" : FOR I = 1 TO 4 : PRINT : NEXT
20 INPUT "ENTER MESSAGE--> "; MS$
30 PRINT : INPUT "HORIZONTAL PLACEMENT (1-40) -> "; H
40 PRINT : INPUT "VERTICAL PLACEMENT (1-25) -> "; V
50 PRINT "{CLR/HOME}"
60 FOR VER = 1 TO V : PRINT : NEXT VER : PRINT TAB(H);
MS$
70 PRINT : PRINT "HIT ANY KEY TO CONTINUE OR 'Q' TO
QUIT ";
80 GET A$ : IF A$ = "" THEN 80
90 IF A$ < > "Q" THEN 10
100 END
```

As you can see, variables can be used with formatting statements. Thus, TAB (H), is read in the same way as TAB(10) or TAB(15) or any other number between 1 and 40. Using the above program, what do you think would happen if you entered "THIS IS A LONG STRING", a HORIZONTAL placement of 39 and a VERTICAL placement of 25? Since the maximum TAB is 40 and the maximum vertical placement is 25, the string (MS$) will go over the boundaries. Go ahead and try it to see what happens. In fact, it would be a good idea to test the limits of TAB and vertical placement with this program to get a clear understanding of their parameters.

Unraveling Strings

Our discussion of strings up to this point has involved "whole" strings. That is, whatever we define a string to be, no matter how long or short, can be considered a "whole" string. For example, if we define R$ as "WALK" then we can consider "WALK" to be the whole of R$. Likewise, if we defined R$ as "A VERY LONG AND WORDY MESSAGE" then, "A VERY LONG AND WORDY MESSAGE" would be the whole string of R$. There will be occasions, however, when we want to use only part of a string or tie several strings together. (When we get into data base programs, we will find this to be very important.) Also, there are applications where we will need to know the length of strings, find the numeric values of strings, and even change strings into numeric variables and back again.

TRUST ME!

I hate to admit it, but when I first learned about all of the commands we are about to discuss, I thought, "Boy, what a waste of time!" It was enough to get the simple material straight, but why in the world would anyone want to chop up strings and put them back together again? If you want only a certain segment of a string, why not simply define it in terms of that segment? And if you want a longer string, then just define it to be longer! Those were my thoughts on the matter of string formatting. However, I have now come to the point where I find it very difficult to even conceive of programming without these powerful commands. So, trust me! String formatting commands are terrific little devices to have, and if you do not see their applicability right away, you will as you begin writing more programs.

String Formatting

We will divide our discussion of string formatting into four parts: 1) Calculating the length of a string; 2) Locating parts of strings; 3) Changing strings to numeric variables and back again; and 4) Tying strings together (concatenation).

Calculating the LENgth of Strings.

Sometimes it is necessary to calculate the length of a string for formatting output. Happily, your COMMODORE-64 is very good at telling you the length of a particular string. By the command, PRINT LEN (A$) you will be given the number of characters, including spaces, your string has. Try the following little program to see how this works:

```
10 PRINT "{CLR/HOME}"
20 INPUT "NAME OF STRING-> "; A$
30 PRINT A$; " HAS "; LEN(A$); " CHARACTERS"
40 PRINT : PRINT " MORE?(Y/N) ";
50 GET AN$ : IF AN$ = "" THEN 50
60 IF AN$ = "Y" THEN 20
```

Now to see a more practical application, we will look at a modified version of the centering routine we used in the last chapter.

```
10 PRINT "{CLR/HOME}"
20 PRINT "ENTER A STRING LESS THAN 40 CHARACTERS"
   : INPUT"-> "; S$
30 PRINT "{CLR/HOME}"
```

40 L = 20 - LEN(S$)/2 : PRINT TAB(L); S$
50 FOR I = 1 TO 20: PRINT : NEXT : : PRINT "HIT ANY KEY
TO CONTINUE OR 'Q' TO QUIT ";
60 GET A$: IF A$ = "" THEN 60
70 IF A$ < > "Q" THEN PRINT "{CLR/HOME}" : GOTO 10
80 END

Now that we can see how to compute the LENgth of a string and then use that LENgth to compute our tabbing, let's see how we can control the input with the LEN command. Suppose you want to write a program which will print out mailing labels, but your labels will hold only 30 characters. You want to make sure all of your entries are 30 or fewer characters long, including spaces. To do this we will write a program which checks the LENgth of a string before it is accepted.

```
10 PRINT "{CLR/HOME}"
20 PRINT "ENTER A NAME LESS THAN 30 CHARACTERS
INCLUDING SPACES"
30 INPUT "DO NOT USE COMMAS -> "; NA$
40 IF LEN (NA$) > 30 THEN GOTO 100 : REM TRAP
50 PRINT : PRINT NA$
60 PRINT : PRINT "ANOTHER NAME?(Y/N) ";
70 GET AN$ : IF AN$ = "" THEN 70
80 IF AN$ < > "Y" THEN END
90 GOTO 10
100 PRINT "{CLR/HOME}" : PRINT "PLEASE USE 30 CHAR-
ACTERS OR LESS "
110 PRINT : GOTO 20
```

Now break the rule!!! Go ahead and enter a string of more than 30 characters to see what happens. (If your computer gets snotty with you, you can always re-program it. It helps to periodically remind it of that fact.) If the program was entered properly, it is impossible to enter a string of more than 30 characters.

From the above examples, you can begin to see how the LEN command can be useful in several ways. There are many other ways that this command can reduce programming time, clarify output, and compute information. The key to understanding its usefulness is to experiment with it and see how other programmers use the same command.

Finding the MIDdle$, LEFT$, and RIGHT$ parts of a string.

Suppose you want to use a single string variable to describe three different conditions, such as "POOR FAIR GOOD", but you want to use only part of that string to describe an outcome. Using MID$, LEFT$ and RIGHT$, it is possible to PRINT only that part of the string you want. For example, the following program lets you use a single string to describe three different conditions:

```
10 PRINT "{CLR/HOME}"
20 X$ = "POOR FAIR GOOD"
30 PRINT "HOW DO YOU FEEL TODAY? (<P>OOR, <F>AIR
   OR <G>OOD)";
40 GET F$ : IF F$ = "" THEN 40
50 IF F$ = "P" THEN PRINT LEFT$(X$,4)
60 IF F$ = "F" THEN PRINT MID$(X$,6,4)
70 IF F$ = "G" THEN PRINT RIGHT$(X$,4)
80 PRINT : PRINT : PRINT "ANOTHER GO?(Y/N) "; :
90 GET AN$ : IF AN$ = "" THEN 90
100 IF AN$ = "Y" THEN 10
```

Let's face it, it would have been easier to simply branch to PRINT 'GOOD' 'FAIR' or 'POOR' and no less efficient. But, no matter, it was for purposes of illustration and not optimizing program organization. Let's see what the new commands do.

COMMAND	MEANING
MID$(A$,N,L)	Finds the portion of A$ beginning at Nth character L characters long.
LEFT$(A$,L)	Finds the portion A$, L characters long starting at the LEFT side of the string.
RIGHT$(A$,L)	Finds the portion of A$, L characters long starting at the RIGHT side of the string.

To give you some immediate experience with these commands, try the
following:

```
W$ = "WHAT A MESS" : PRINT LEFT$(W$,4) <RETURN>
G$ = "BURLESQUE" : PRINT MID$(G$,4,3) <RETURN>
X$ = "A PLACE IN SPACE" : PRINT RIGHT$(X$,5) : PRINT
RIGHT$(X$,3)
<RETURN>
```

Another trick with partial strings is to assign parts of one string to another
string. For example:

```
10 PRINT "{CLR/HOME}"
20 BIG$ = "LONG LONG AGO AND FAR FAR AWAY"
30 LITTLE$ = MID$(BIG$,11,3)
40 AWY$ = RIGHT$(BIG$,4)
50 LG$ = LEFT$(BIG$,4)
60 PRINT : PRINT : PRINT AWY$;" ";LG$;" ";LITTLE$
70 REM BEFORE YOU RUN IT, SEE IF YOU CAN GUESS THE
MESSAGE.
```

For an interesting effect, try the following little program:

```
10 PRINT "{CLR/HOME}" : FOR I = 1 TO 10 : PRINT : NEXT
20 INPUT "YOUR NAME--> "; NA$
30 FOR I = LEN(NA$) TO 1 STEP -1 : PRINT MID$(NA$,I,1); :
NEXT I
40 FOR I = 1 TO 1000 : NEXT I : REM DELAY LOOP
45 REM ** LINE 50 USES THE NON-SHIFTED CLR/HOME KEY
**
46 REM ** NOTE HOW IT FUNCTIONS TO PLACE THE CUR-
SOR VERTICALLY **
47 REM ** IN CONJUNCTION WITH THE LOOP **
50 PRINT "{HOME}" : FOR V = 1 TO 11 :PRINT : NEXT V
55 REM ** IN LINE 60 'K LOOP' SLOWS IT DOWN FOR SLOW
MOTION EFFECT **
60 FOR I = 1 TO LEN(NA$) : PRINT MID$(NA$, I,1); : FOR K
= 1 TO 50 : NEXT K : NEXT I
70 FOR VT = 1 TO 5 : PRINT : NEXT VT: PRINT TAB (5);
"WANNA DO IT AGAIN?(Y/N) ";
80 GET AN$: IF AN$ = "" THEN 80
90 IF AN$ = "Y" THEN 10
```

Now you have probably been wondering ever since you got your computer how to make it print your name backwards. Well, now you know! (If your name is BOB you probably didn't notice it was printed backwards - try ROBERT.) Actually, the above exercise did a couple of things besides goofing off. First, it is a demonstration of how loops and partial strings (or substrings) can be used together for formatting output. Second, we showed how output could be slowed down for either an interesting effect or simply to give the user time to see what's happening.

Since we're on the topic of speed, let's learn how to use your COMMO-DORE-64's clock. Remember we pointed out that TI$ was a "reserved variable," and now we will see why. Try the following in the Immediate Mode:

     TI$ = "101030" <RETURN>

Now wait a few seconds and enter,

     PRINT TI$ <RETURN>

The value of TI$ changed from 101030 to something else! If you waited for just a few seconds, 101030 changed to 101050 or somewhere in that range. To see what is happening, let's break it down into hours, minutes and seconds.

10 10 30 = 10 hours 10 minutes 30 seconds.

We'd say that time is 10:10 and 30 seconds on a normal clock. Well, that's exactly what TI$ does. It ticks off the seconds, then minutes and finally hours. To see this better, let's make a little clock program.

```
10 PRINT "{CLR/HOME}" : PRINT "COMMODORE-64 CLOCK"
20 FOR I = 1 TO 4 : PRINT : NEXT : PRINT "ENTER TIME (00
HRS 00 MINS 00 SECS)"
30 INPUT TI$
40 PRINT "{CLR/HOME}"
50 PRINT "{HOME}" : FOR I=1 TO 10 : PRINT : NEXT : PRINT
"COMMODORE TIME-> ";TI$ : GOTO 50
```

When you run this program, be sure to enter all 6 digits for hours, minutes and seconds. For example, if the time you want to enter is 8:14, enter 081400, not just 814.

Besides using TI$ for a clock to display time on your screen, you can also use it for a timer in your programs. By first setting a value for TI$ and then checking it in your program, you can have timing for responses. The following is a simple math game which adds the element of time:

```
10 PRINT "{CLR/HOME}": FOR I = 1 TO 5 : PRINT :
NEXT : TI$ = "000000"
20 INPUT "ENTER 1ST NUMBER->"; A
30 INPUT "ENTER 2ND NUMBER->"; B
40 PRINT : PRINT "WHAT IS"; A ; "+"; B;
50 INPUT C
60 IF A + B < > C THEN 200
70 IF TI$ > "000010" THEN GOTO 100
80 PRINT : PRINT "THAT'S RIGHT!!!!" : FOR X = 1 TO 1000 :
NEXT : GOTO 10
100 PRINT "{CLR/HOME}" : PRINT : PRINT  "YOU RAN OUT
OF TIME!"
110 FOR TM = 1 TO 1000 : NEXT TM : GOTO 10
200 PRINT "THAT'S NOT QUITE RIGHT" : INPUT "PRESS
RETURN TO CONTINUE";CR
210 GOTO 10
```

Examine the program carefully. Note how the time is checked in line 70 and how it is reset to "000000" each time the process is restarted.

Changing Strings To Numbers and Back Again

Now we're going to learn about changing strings to numbers and numbers to strings. If you're like me, when I first found out about these commands, I thought they were pretty useless. After all, if you want a string use a string variable, and if you want a number use a numeric variable. Simple enough, but again, once you understand their value, you wonder how you could do without them. To get started, let's RUN the following program:

```
10 PRINT "{CLR/HOME}"
20 FOR I = 1 TO 5 : READ NA$(I) : NEXT I
30 FOR I = 1 TO 5
40 X(I) = VAL(RIGHT$(NA$(I),1))
50 NEXT I
60 FOR I = 1 TO 5 : PRINT "OVERTIME PAY = $"; X(I) * (1.5 *
7) : NEXT I
70 DATA SMITH 7, JONES 8, MCKNAP 6, JOHNSON 2,
KELLY 3
```

Using DATA which were originally in a string format, we were able to change a portion of that string array to a numeric array. By making such a conversion, we were able to use our mathematical operations on line 60 to figure out the overtime pay for someone receiving time and a half at seven dollars ($7) an hour. Well, that's pretty interesting, but we don't have a list of who got what and the total overtime paid! Why don't you try it yourself. Change the program so that everyone's name appears with the amount of overtime they received and a total overtime paid. (Hint: You are looking for the substring LEFT$ (NA$(I), LEN (NA$(I)) − 2) since you want to drop the number and space after each name.) When you get it, write me a letter to show me how you figured it out.

It always helps to do a few immediate exercises with a new command to get the right feel, so try these:

```
A$ = "123" : PRINT VAL(A$) + 11 <RETURN>
Q$ = "99.5" : PRINT VAL(Q$) * 7 <RETURN>
SALE$ = "44.95" : PRINT "ON SALE AT HALF PRICE ->$";
VAL(SALE$) / 2 <RETURN>
DO$ = "$103.88" : DN$ = "$18.34" : PRINT VAL
(RIGHT$(DO$,6))
 + VAL (RIGHT$(DN$,5)) <RETURN>
```

NOTE: Since you may want to SAVE the above examples on tape or disk, just add line numbers and SAVE them as little programs.

From Numbers to Strings

All right, now let's go the other way. We saw why we might want to change
strings to numbers, but we may also want to change numbers to strings.
To make the conversion we use the STR$ command. For example, look
at the following program:

```
10 PRINT "{CLR/HOME}"
20 PRINT "ENTER A NUMBER WITH 5 DIGITS ": INPUT "
AFTER THE DECIMAL POINT " ; A
30 A$ = STR$(A)
40 PRINT : PRINT LEFT$ (A$,4)
```

As you can see, you have truncated the number to 3 characters including
the decimal point. Change LEFT$ to RIGHT$ in line 40 and you will get the
rightmost 4 <not 3> characters of the string. LEFT$ actually gives you 4
characters also, but the leftmost character   is a space when the number is
positive and a minus sign when negative. Now, let's do some in the
immediate mode to get the idea firmly into your mind, and a little later we will
do something very practical with these commands.

```
A = 5.00 : A$ = STR$(A) : PRINT A$ <RETURN>
V = 2345 : V$ = STR$(V) : PRINT V$ <RETURN>
BUCKS = 22.36 : BUCKS$ = STR$(BUCKS) : PRINT
LEFT$(BUCKS$,2) <RETURN>
```

Remember these commands. When you are dealing with decimal points you will often find them handy.

Tying Strings Together: Concatenation

We have seen how we can take a portion of a string and PRINT it to the screen. Now, we will tie strings together. This is called *CONCATENATION* and is accomplished by using the " + " sign with strings. For example:

```
10 PRINT "{CLR/HOME}"
20 INPUT "YOUR FIRST NAME -> "; NF$
30 INPUT "YOUR LAST NAME -> "; NL$
40 NA$ = NF$ + NL$
50 PRINT NA$
```

A little messy, huh? However, you can see how NF$ and NL$ were tied together into a single larger string. Now, change line 40 to read

```
40 NA$ = NF$ + " " + NL$
```

This time when you RUN the program, your name will turn out fine. Not only did we concatenate string variables, we also concatenated strings themselves. For example, it is perfectly all right to do the following:

```
PRINT "ONE" + "ONE" <RETURN>
```

Now there isn't much you can do with ONEONE, but we can see the principle of operation with concatenating strings.

One of the problems with the way your COMMODORE-64 formats numbers is that it drops 0's off the end. For example, try the following:

    PRINT 19.80
    PRINT 5.00

In dealing with dollars and cents, this can be a real pain in the neck, and it doesn't look very good. So, using concatenation and our VAL and STR$ commands, let's see if we can fix that.

```
10 PRINT "{CLR/HOME}"
20 PRINT "BE SURE TO INCLUDE ALL CENTS!" : PRINT : PRINT
30 INPUT "HOW MUCH SPENT?-> $"; S
40 T = T + S
50 T$ = STR$(T)
60 T$ = "000" + T$ : REM THIS IS TO INSURE THAT LEN(T$) IS LONG ENOUGH
70 IF MID$ (T$, (LEN (T$) - 1),1) = "." THEN T$ = T$ + "0" : GOTO 90
80 IF MID$ (T$, (LEN (T$) -2),1) < > "." THEN T$ = T$ + ".00"
90 PRINT : PRINT : PRINT "YOU NOW HAVE SPENT $"; RIGHT$(T$, LEN(T$) -3)
100 PRINT "PRESS ANY KEY TO CONTINUE OR 'Q' TO QUIT";
110 GET R$ : IF R$ = "" THEN 110
120 IF R$ = "Q" THEN END
130 GOTO 10
```

This may look pretty complicated, but let's break it down to see what has been done.

1. We entered numeric variables in line 30 and computed their sum in line 40.

2. The sum represented by T was then converted to a string variable T$ in line 50.

3. In line 60 we "padded" T$ with three 0's to give it a minimum length we will need in lines 70 and 80.

4. Line 70 computes the second from the last character in T$. If that character is a decimal point (.) then we know it must be a figure which dropped off the last cent column. (e.g. 5.4, 19.5, etc.). So we tack on a 0, and jump to line 90.

5. Line 80 computes the third from the last character, and if it is not a decimal point (.) then we know it must have dropped all the cents completely - an even dollar number. So we tack on the decimal point and two 0's (.00).

6. Finally, in line 90 we print out our results but first dropping the "padding" we added in line 60 using RIGHT$. The statement 'LEN (T$)-3' computes the length of T$ and subtracts three, the unwanted three 0's.

All of this may seem a bit complicated just to get our 0's back, but actually, the entire process was done in 5 lines (50 through 90). SAVE the program, and when you need those 0's in your output, just include those lines! (Be careful, though, this will not work with subtraction when you get below $1!).

Setting Up Data Entry

Now that we have a firm grip on numerous commands, it is time we begin thinking seriously about organizing our programs. First we must arrange our data entry in a manner that we ourselves and others can understand. This involves blocking elements of our program and deciding what variables and arrays we will be using. Also, when we enter data, we want to make sure that we are entering the correct type of data; so we have to set "traps" so that any input which is over a certain length or amount can be checked against our parameters. Let's look at a way to make our strings a certain length (no shorter or longer than a length we want). We've already discussed how to keep strings to a maximum length, so let's see how to keep them to a minimum as well. This latter process is referred to as "padding."

```
10 PRINT "{CLR/HOME}"
20 FOR I = 1 TO 8 : PRINT : NEXT I : INPUT "YOUR COMPANY-
->"; CM$
30 IF LEN(CM$) < = 10 THEN 70
40 IF LEN(CM$) > 10 THEN PRINT "10 OR FEWER CHAR-
ACTERS PLEASE" : REM TRAP FOR TOO LONG A NAME
42 REM PRESS THE CTRL AND 9 KEYS SIMULTANEOUSLY
{CTRL-9} IN LINE 45
45 PRINT :PRINT "{CTRL-9}HIT ANY KEY TO CONTINUE-> ";
50 GET A$ : IF A$ = "" THEN 50
60 GOTO 10
70 IF LEN(CM$) < 10 THEN CM$ = CM$ + "X" : GOTO 70 :
REM PADDING
```

```
80 PRINT "{CLR/HOME}" : FOR I = 1 TO 8 : PRINT : NEXT :
PRINT "THE COMPUTER HAS DECIDED THAT "
90 PRINT CM$; " SHOULD GIVE YOU A RAISE!"
```

Now if YOUR COMPANY <CM$> is less than 10 characters, you will see some "X's" stuck on the end. These were put there to show you how padding works. Now change the "X" to " " <a space> in line 70 and see what happens. Go ahead. The second time you run the program, if your company's name is less than 10 characters, there are a lot of blank spaces after the company name. To remove the spaces, we would enter:

```
75  IF  MID$(CM$,LEN(CM$),1)  =  " "  THEN  CM$  =
LEFT$(CM$,(LEN(CM$)-1): GOTO 75
```

Setting Up Data Manipulation

Once you have organized your input, the next major step is performing computations with your data. There are essentially two kinds of data manipulation you will deal with:

1. NUMERIC - Manipulating numeric data with mathematical operations.

2. STRING - Manipulating strings with concatenation and sub-string commands.

Most of the string manipulations are for setting up input or output, so we will concentrate on manipulating numeric data. We will use a simple example which keeps track of three manipulations: (1) additions (2) subtractions and (3) running balance. This will be our checkbook program we started earlier.

```
10 PRINT "{CLR/HOME}"
20 REM ### BEGIN INPUT & HEADER BLOCK ###
30 CB$ = " =COMPUTER CHECK-BOOK= ": L = 20 - LEN
(CB$) / 2: PRINT TAB(L);"(CTRL-9)"; CB$ : REM =HEADER=
40 FOR I = 1 TO 4 : PRINT : NEXT : INPUT "ENTER YOUR
CURRENT BALANCE-> $";BA
50  PRINT : PRINT : PRINT "1. ENTER DEPOSITS" : PRINT
 : PRINT "2. DEDUCT CHECKS"
55 PRINT : PRINT "3. EXIT"
60 FOR I = 1 TO 7 : PRINT : NEXT : PRINT "(CTRL-9) CHOOSE
BY NUMBER "; : INPUT A
```

```
70 ON A GOTO 100,200,400
80 GOTO 60: REM TRAP
90 REM END OF INPUT BLOCK
100 REM ### DATA MANIPULATION ROUTINE NO. 1 ###
110 PRINT"{CLR/HOME}" : FOR I = 1 TO 6 : PRINT : NEXT:
INPUT "ENTER AMOUNT OF DEPOSIT $";DP
120 BA = BA + DP: REM RUNNING BALANCE
130 PRINT : PRINT : PRINT "YOU NOW HAVE $";BA;" IN YOUR
ACCOUNT"
140 PRINT : INPUT "(CTRL-9)MORE DEPOSITS? (Y/N) "; AN$
150 IF AN$ = "Y" THEN 110
160 PRINT : INPUT "WOULD YOU LIKE TO DEDUCT CHECKS?
(Y/N) ";  AN$
170 IF AN$ = "N" THEN GOTO 400
180 IF AN$ = "Y" THEN GOTO 200
190 PRINT"{CLR/HOME}" : GOTO 160: REM TRAP & END OF
DATA MANIPULATION ROUTINE NO.1
200 REM ### DATA MANIPULATION ROUTINE NO. 2 ###
210 PRINT"{CLR/HOME}" : FOR I = 1 TO 6 : PRINT : NEXT:
INPUT "ENTER AMOUNT OF CHECK $";CK
220 BA = BA - CK: REM RUNNING BALANCE
230 PRINT : PRINT "YOU NOW HAVE $";BA;" IN YOUR
ACCOUNT"
240 PRINT : INPUT "MORE CHECKS? (Y/N) - 'Q' TO QUIT ";
AN$
250 IF AN$ = "Y" THEN 210
260 IF AN$ = "Q" THEN 400
270 PRINT : INPUT "ANY DEPOSITS? (Y/N) ";  AD$
280 IF AD$ = "Y" THEN 100
290 GOTO 240: REM TRAP & END OF DATA MANIPULATION
BLOCK NO. 2
400 REM ### TERMINATION BLOCK ###
410 PRINT"{CLR/HOME}" : FOR I = 1 TO 400: PRINT "$";:
NEXT
420 PRINT "YOU NOW HAVE A BALANCE OF $";BA
```

This program is designed to provide a simple illustration of how to block
data manipulation. However, there are some problems with it in the output.
We are not getting the 0's on the end of our balance! This is an "output"
problem we will discuss in the following section, but before we continue,
make sure you understand how we blocked the data manipulation. We
used only three variables:

```
BA = BALANCE
CK = CHECK
DP = DEPOSIT
```

When we subtracted a check, we simply subtracted CK from BA; and
when we entered a deposit, we added DP to BA. In this way we were able
to keep a running balance and, at the very end, BA was the total of all
deposits and checks. By keeping it simple and in blocks we were able to
jump around and still keep everything straight.

Organizing Output

Let's go back to our program and repair it so that our balance will have
the 0's where they belong. This is essentially a problem of output because
all of the computations have been done. They correctly tell us our balance,
but it doesn't look right with the missing 0's. However, we would rather not
have to enter the lines for converting our balance into a string variable
every time the running balance is printed. Therefore, we will put the subroutine for our conversion in a block. Looking at our COMPUTER CHECK
BOOK program, it just so happens that there is a block available in the
300's - our luck is with us! We'll use that block to format our output.

```
300 REM ### FORMAT OUTPUT ###
310 BA = BA + .001:PLACE = 1:BA$ = STR$ (BA): IF BA <
.001 THEN BA$ = "0.00": GOTO 340
320 IF MID$ (BA$,PLACE,1) < > "." THEN PLACE = PLACE
+ 1: GOTO 320
330 BA$ = LEFT$ (BA$,PLACE + 2)
340 RETURN
350 REM END OF OUTPUT BLOCK
```

Now we simply change a few lines in our program so that when there is
an output of our balance, it will jump to the subroutine between lines 300
and 350 and then RETURN to output BA$. The following lines in our
COMPUTER CHECKBOOK program should be changed and/or added:

```
125 GOSUB 300
130 PRINT : PRINT : PRINT "YOU NOW HAVE $"; BA$; "IN
YOUR ACCOUNT"
225 GOSUB 300
230 PRINT : PRINT "YOU NOW HAVE $"; BA$; " IN YOUR
ACCOUNT"
415 GOSUB 300
420 PRINT "YOU NOW HAVE A BALANCE OF $"; BA$
```

Now if you put everything together properly, you should have a handy little program for working with your checkbook. Just to make sure you got everything, here's the complete program with all the subroutines and changes we made:

```
10 PRINT "{CLR/HOME}"
20 REM ### BEGIN INPUT & HEADER BLOCK ###
30 CB$ = " =COMPUTER CHECK-BOOK= ": L = 20 - LEN
(CB$) / 2: PRINT TAB(L);"(CTRL-9)"; CB$ : REM =HEADER=
40 FOR I = 1 TO 4 : PRINT : NEXT : INPUT "ENTER YOUR
CURRENT BALANCE-> $";BA
50 PRINT : PRINT : PRINT  "1. ENTER DEPOSITS" : PRINT :
PRINT "2.  DEDUCT CHECKS"
55 PRINT : PRINT "3. EXIT"
60 FOR I = 1 TO 7 : PRINT : NEXT : PRINT "(CTRL-9) CHOOSE
BY NUMBER "; : INPUT A
70 ON A GOTO 100,200,400
80 GOTO 60: REM TRAP
90 REM END OF INPUT BLOCK
100 REM ### DATA MANIPULATION ROUTINE NO. 1 ###
110 PRINT"{CLR/HOME}" : FOR I = 1 TO 6 : PRINT : NEXT:
INPUT "ENTER AMOUNT OF DEPOSIT $";DP
120 BA = BA + DP: REM RUNNING BALANCE
125 GOSUB 300
130 PRINT : PRINT : PRINT "YOU NOW HAVE $";BA$;" IN
YOUR ACCOUNT"
140 PRINT : INPUT "(CTRL-9)MORE DEPOSITS? (Y/N) "; AN$
150 IF AN$ = "Y" THEN 110
160 PRINT : INPUT "WOULD YOU LIKE TO DEDUCT CHECKS?
(Y/N) "; AN$
170 IF AN$ = "N" THEN GOTO 400
180 IF AN$ = "Y" THEN GOTO 200
190 PRINT"{CLR/HOME}" : GOTO 160: REM TRAP & END OF
DATA MANIPULATION ROUTINE NO.1
200 REM ### DATA MANIPULATION ROUTINE NO. 2 ###
210 PRINT"{CLR/HOME}" : FOR I = 1 TO 6 : PRINT : NEXT:
INPUT "ENTER AMOUNT OF CHECK $";CK
220 BA = BA - CK: REM RUNNING BALANCE
225 GOSUB 300
230 PRINT : PRINT "YOU NOW HAVE $";BA$;" IN YOUR
ACCOUNT"
240 PRINT : INPUT "MORE CHECKS? (Y/N) - 'Q' TO QUIT ";
AN$
250 IF AN$ = "Y" THEN 210
```

```
260 IF AN$ = "Q" THEN 400
270 PRINT : INPUT "ANY DEPOSITS? (Y/N) ";  AD$
280 IF AD$ = "Y" THEN 100
290 GOTO 240: REM TRAP & END OF DATA MANIPULATION
BLOCK NO. 2
300 REM ### FORMAT OUTPUT ###
310 BA = BA + .001:PLACE = 1:BA$ = STR$ (BA): IF BA <
.001 THEN BA$ = "0.00": GOTO 340
320 IF MID$ (BA$,PLACE,1) < > "." THEN PLACE = PLACE
+ 1: GOTO 320
330 BA$ = LEFT$ (BA$,PLACE + 2)
340 RETURN
350 REM END OF OUTPUT BLOCK
400 REM ### TERMINATION BLOCK ###
410 PRINT"{CLR/HOME}" : FOR I = 1 TO 400: PRINT "$";:
NEXT
415 GOSUB 300 : REM NOTE THAT A 'GOSUB' CAN GO BACK-
WARDS IN LINE NUMBERS!
420 PRINT "YOU NOW HAVE A BALANCE OF $";BA$
```

Scroll Control!

One of the big problems in output occurs when you have long lists which
will scroll right off the screen. For example, the output of the following
program will kick the output right out the top of the screen:

```
10 PRINT "{CLR/HOME}"
20 FOR I = 1 TO 100 : PRINT I : NEXT
```

Instead of numbers, suppose you have a list of names you have sorted
or some other output you wanted to see before they zipped off the top of
the screen. Depending on the desired output, screen format and so forth
there are several different ways to control the scroll. Consider the following:

```
10 PRINT "{CLR/HOME}"
20 FOR I = 1 TO 100
30 IF I = 20 THEN GOSUB 100
40 IF I = 40 THEN GOSUB 100
50 IF I = 60 THEN GOSUB 100
60 IF I = 80 THEN GOSUB 100
70 PRINT I : NEXT I
80 END
100 PRINT : PRINT :PRINT "(CTRL-9) HIT ANY KEY TO CON-
```

        TINUE " ;
        110 GET A$: IF A$ = "" THEN 110
        120 PRINT "{CLR/HOME}" : RETURN

REMEMBER!! You, not the computer, are in CONTROL! You can have your output any way you want it. To use more of the screen, you could have the output tabbed to another column after the vertical screen is filled. For example:

        10 PRINT "{CLR/HOME}"
        20 FOR I = 1 TO 40
        30 IF I > 20 THEN GOSUB 100
        50 PRINT I : NEXT I
        80 END
        100 PRINT "{HOME}" : FOR J = 1 TO (I-20) : PRINT : NEXT J:
        PRINT TAB (10);
        110 RETURN

You get the idea. Format your ouput in a manner which best uses the screen and your needs and get that scroll under control!

Summary

The formatting of programs makes the difference between a useful and a not-so-useful application of your computer. The extent to which your program is well organized and clear, the better the chances are for simple yet effective programming. Formatting is more than an exercise in making your input/output fancy or interesting. It is a matter of communication between your COMMODORE-64 and you! After all, if you can't make heads or tails of what your computer has computed, the best calculations in the world are of absolutely no use.

In the same way it is important to have your computer tell you what you want, it is also important to write your programs so that you and others can understand what is happening. By using "blocks" it is easier to organize and later understand exactly what each part of your program does. Obviously, it is possible to write programs sequentially so that each command and subroutine is in an ascending order of line numbers; but to do so means that you will have to repeat simple and/or complex operations which could be better handled as subroutines. Also, it will be considerably more difficult to locate bugs and make the appropriate changes. In other words, by using a structured approach to programming, you make it simpler not more difficult.

Finally, you should begin to see why there are commands for substrings and all the fuss about TABs. These are handy tools for organizing the various parts in a manner which gives you complete control over your computer's output. What may at first seem like a petty, even silly, command in COMMODORE-64 BASIC, upon a useful application, can be appreciated as an excellent tool. Therefore, as we delve deeper into your computer, look at the variety of commands as mechanisms of more efficient and ultimately simpler control and not a complex "gobbleygook" of "computerese" for geniuses. After all, if you've come this far, you should realize that what you know now looked like the work of "computer whizzes" when you first began.

CHAPTER 6

Some Advanced Topics

(But Not Too Difficult Once You Get To Know Them)

Introduction

The topics of this chapter are more "code like" and contain the kinds of commands that look frightening. At least that's how I interpreted them when I first saw them. Many of the functions can be done with commands we already know, but many cannot. Still others, as we will see, can be accomplished better using these new commands. Like so much else you have seen in this book, what at first may appear to be "impossible" is really quite simple once you get the idea. More importantly, by playing with the commands, you can quickly learn their use.

The first thing we will learn about is the ASCII code. ASCII (pronounced ASS-KEY) stands for the AMERICAN STANDARD CODE for INFORMATION INTERCHANGE. Essentially, this is a set of numbers that have been standardized to mean certain characters. In COMMODORE-64 BASIC the CHR$ (character string) command ties into ASCII and can be used to directly output ASCII. As we will see, the CHR$ command is very useful for outputting special characters.

The next commands have to do with directly accessing locations in your computer's memory. The first, POKE, puts values into memory and the second, PEEK, looks into memory addresses and returns the values there. We will examine several different uses of these two commands. These commands are essential for producing certain types of graphics and sound.

The ASCII Code and CHR$ Functions

In a couple of places we have used control characters in programs, such as CTRL-9. In the program all we saw was something like the following:

```
PRINT "{INVERSE R}": REM CTRL-9
```

What that means is that we enter the CTRL-9 between the quote marks, but an inverse "R" is there. Unfortunately, we cannot see the CTRL-9 when we list our program to printer or screen; so we have to use a REM statement to let us know what's there or remember that an inverse "R" is really a CTRL-9. Another way to access any characters we want, including control characters, is to use CHR$ commands and the ASCII code. In APPENDIX A there is a complete listing of ASCII which you will want to examine. Whenever we want to access a character, we just enter the CHR$ and the decimal value of the character we want. For example enter the following:

```
PRINT CHR$(65) <RETURN>
```

You got an "A". That's simple enough and not too interesting. On the other hand, try the following little program, and I'll bet you couldn't do it without using the CHR$ function:

```
10 PRINT CHR$(147) : REM USES ASCII FOR CLR/HOME
20 QU$ = CHR$(34) : REM USES ASCII VALUE FOR QUOTE
MARKS
30 FOR I = 1 TO 20 : PRINT : NEXT : PRINT CHR$(18);"HIT
ANY KEY TO CONTINUE OR ";
40 PRINT QU$ ; "Q" ; QU$ ; " TO QUIT ";
50 GET AN$ : IF AN$ = "" THEN 50
60 IF AN$ = "Q" THEN END
70 GOTO 10
```

RUN the program and look carefully. Note the quotes around the Q. If we tried to PRINT a quote mark, the computer would think it got a command to begin printing a string. However, but defining QU$ as CHR$(34) we were able to slip in the quote marks and not confuse the output! (Just for fun, see if you can do that without using the CHR$ command.) Also, did you notice how we began the program? Instead of using the CLR/HOME key, we used CHR$(147). We did not have to put in the quote (") marks around CHR$(147) as we did with CLR/HOME. Likewise, we used CHR$(18) instead of a CTRL-9 to set the inverse mode. To see what different characters you have available, RUN the following program:

```
10 PRINT CHR$(147)
20 FOR I = 32 TO 127 : PRINT CHR$(I); : NEXT
30 FOR I = 158 TO 191 : PRINT CHR$(I) ; : NEXT
```

Voila! There you have all of your symbols. Before we go on, though, let's
see some other symbols simply by pressing two keys. Hold down the
COMMODORE key (in the lower left hand corner of your keyboard) and
press the SHIFT key. The first set of letters were printed in lower case and
the symbols, beginning with the "spade" changed to upper case letters.
Thus, depending on whether or not the lower case letters are "on" or "off,"
CHR$s will output different symbols. Now, to watch funny things happen
to your screen RUN the following program.

```
10 PRINT CHR$(147)
20 FOR I = 0 TO 31
30 PRINT CHR$(I) ; : NEXT
```

Not much happened since in that range of ASCII (from 0 to 31) you ran
through the control characters. In fact, your system "locked up," and you
will have to press RUN/STOP and RESTORE together to get everything
back. To get used to your increased power over your computer, try the
following little programs:

```
10 PRINT CHR$(147)
20 LB$ = CHR$ (54) : RB$ = CHR$(52)
30 CO$ = "COMMODORE" + CHR$(45) + LB$ + RB$
40 L = 20 - LEN (CO$)/2 : PRINT SPC(L); CO$
50 FOR I = 1 TO 20 : PRINT CHR$(32) : NEXT
```

```
10 PRINT CHR$(147)
20 PRINT CHR$(18); CHR$(28); : FOR I = 1 TO 35 : PRINT
CHR$(32) ; : NEXT
30 PRINT CHR$(5) : REM BEFORE YOU RUN THIS, SEE IF
YOU CAN FIGURE OUT WHAT WILL HAPPEN
```

On the last program, you will get an idea of the use of CHR$ commands
with graphics. The red bar was created using CHR$(32), a space, after
the color red had been set with CHR$(18) <CTRL-9> and CHR$(28)
<CTRL-3>. In the next chapter on graphics, we will use the CHR$ com-
mand a good deal in creating pictures, charts and graphs. (By the way,
to reset everything to normal, use the RUN/STOP and RESTORE keys.)

The following program is a handy little device for printing out all of the
CHR$ values to screen. Save it to tape or disk to use as a handy reference
guide to look up CHR$ values and symbols.

```
10 PRINT CHR$(147)
20 GOSUB 300
30 FOR I = 33 TO 99
40 IF I = 34 THEN GOTO 400
50 PRINT I; ". = "; CHR$(I),
60 NEXT
70 PRINT : PRINT "HIT ANY KEY TO CONTINUE";
80 GET A$ : IF A$ = "" THEN 80
90 PRINT CHR$ (147)
100 GOSUB 300
110 FOR I = 100 TO 127: PRINT I;". = " ; CHR$ (I), : NEXT
120 FOR I = 161 TO 191 : PRINT I; ". = "; CHR$(I), : NEXT
130 PRINT : PRINT : END
300 FOR I = 1 TO 4 : PRINT " CHR$ / S", : NEXT
310 RETURN
400 PRINT I; ". = "; "''", : REM THERE ARE 2 SHIFT 7'S
BETWEEN THE QUOTE MARKS
410 GOTO 60
```

The program, CHR$ MAP, can be used as a handy reference for you to look up the CHR$ values of different symbols. You may have noticed that the program branches to a subroutine at line 400 if I = 34. The reason for that is because once a quotation mark - CHR$(34) - is encountered, inverse brackets will be printed in the rest of the output. To avoid that, we made a "phony quote mark" using two apostrophes (SHIFT 7). This left a gap between 34 and 35, but it looks a lot better than all those inverse brackets! Also, we left out CHR$ values which would either lock up the display, clear the screen, change the colors or somehow mess up the output. See if you can make a program which will include useful CHR$ values (such as CTRL-9 and colors) but not destroy the output.

POKES and PEEKS:
Looking Inside Your Commodore-64's Memory

At first you won't have too many uses for POKES and PEEKS, but as you begin exploring the full range of your computer's capacity, they will be used more and more. Basically, a POKE command places a value into a given memory location and a PEEK command returns the value stored in that location. For example, try the following:

POKE 2048, 255 : PRINT PEEK (2048) <RETURN>

You should have gotten "255" since the POKE command entered that value into location 2048 and PRINT PEEK (2048) printed out the value of that address. That's relatively simple, but more is going on than storage of numbers.

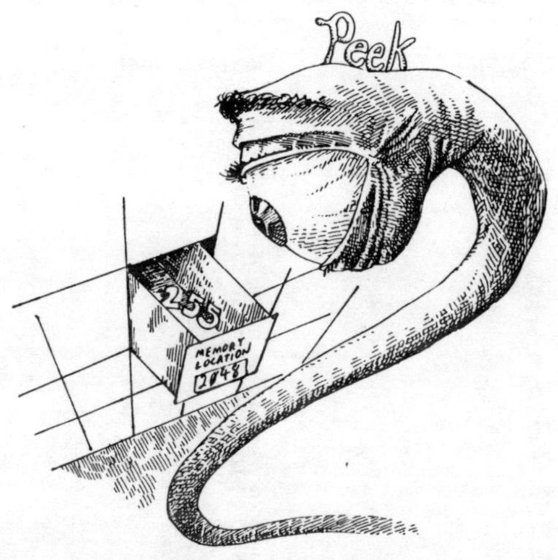

The key importance of POKE and PEEK involves what occurs in a given memory location when a given value is entered. In some locations nothing other than the storage of the number will occur, as in our example above. However, with other memory locations, very precise events occur. What we will do in the remainder of this section is to examine some of the more useful locations for POKEing and PEEKing in your COMMODORE-64. We will not be getting into the more complex elements of POKEs and PEEKs, however.

A TALE OF TWO NUMBER SYSTEMS

When using POKEs and PEEKs, we use decimal numbers for accessing locations. However, much of what is written about special locations in your PROGRAMMER'S REFERENCE GUIDE available for your COMMODORE-64 is written in HEXADECIMAL, generally referred to as HEX. Since we've used decimal notations for counting all our lives, it seems to be a "natural" way of doing things. However, decimal is simply a "base 10" method of counting and we could use a base of anything we wanted. For reasons I won't get into here "base 16," called HEXADECIMAL, is an easier way to think about using a computer's memory, and that's why so much of the notation we see is in HEX. HEX is counted in the same way as decimal except it is done in groups of 16, and it uses alphanumeric characters instead of just numeric ones. You can usually tell if a number is HEX since they are typically preceded by a dollar-sign (e.g. $45 is not the same as decimal 45), and often there are alphabetic characters mixed in with numbers. (e.g. FC58, AAB, 12C). The following is a list of decimal and hexadecimal numbers.

Decimal	Hexadecimal
0	$0
1	$1
2	$2
3	$3
4	$4
5	$5
6	$6
7	$7
8	$8
9	$9
10	$A
11	$B
12	$C
13	$D
14	$E
15	$F
16	$10

As you can see, instead of starting with double digit numbers at 10, hexadecimal begins double digits at decimal 16 with a $10. In the major memory locations of interest in your COMMODORE-64 PROGRAMMER'S REFERENCE GUIDE, both the decimal and hexadecimal numbers are given.

A ROTTEN TRICK!!

When you start POKEing and PEEKing into different locations of your COMMODORE-64, you will not always get what you expect. In the decimal addresses from 2048 through 40959, you will be pretty safe since this is the User Basic area. However, other locations are the "homes" of special routines which will react directly to anything POKEd into them. For example, if you POKE 768,255 : PRINT PEEK (768), your machine will lock up, and not even RUN/ STOP and RESTORE will unlock it. You have to turn your computer off to free it up. Now if you slipped that into one of your programs and gave it to a friend, it would lock up his machine, and that would be a Rotten Trick! Of course, you wouldn't ever do anything like that. Would you?

Now let's take a look at some places to POKE. We will begin with your text screen.

Poking the Text Screen

Another use of POKEs is to enter a character to a location on your text screen. Each character has a different value between 0 and 255. Your screen can be envisioned as a set of addresses on a 40 by 25 grid beginning with decimal location 1024 and ending at 2023. That gives you exactly 1000 locations on your screen where you can place text. The addresses are contiguous, and by using FOR-NEXT loops it is a simple matter to enter sequential lines of text. Or, using POKEs, you can put text anywhere on the screen you want. To get an idea of what you will see, run this short program, then try the following POKEs:

```
10  PRINT CHR$(147) : B = 55296 : FOR I = B TO B + 999 :
    POKE I,1 : NEXT

POKE 1190, 1 : POKE 1191, 129 <RETURN>
FOR I = 1880 TO 1890 : POKE I, 81 : NEXT  <RETURN>
FOR I = 1240 TO (1240 + 255) : POKE I,  I - 1240 :
    NEXT <RETURN>
```

The first line showed different addresses for normal and inverse "A" located at adjacent addresses. The next exercise used a sequence of addresses from 1880 to 1890 and put in a white ball at each location. Finally, the third exercise used adjacent memory locations to insert a sequence of ASCII characters.

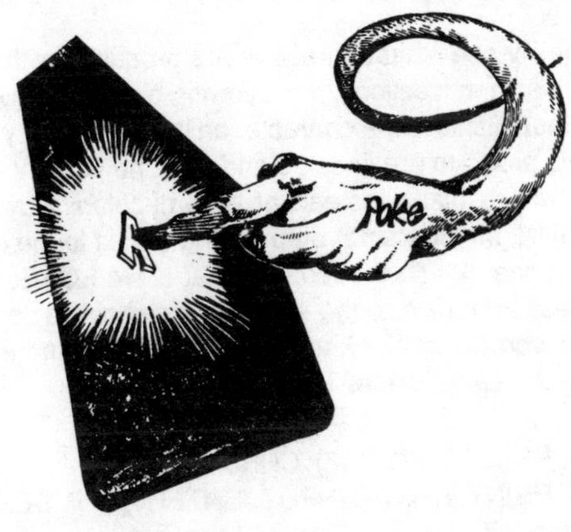

The following program will introduce you to the concept of an "offset" in programming. Bascially, an offset is a number which will add or subtract a specified value. There are two different offsets in the program to note. The first is "127," used in determining the maximum address for the loops beginning in lines 20 and 40. Since we want to POKE in 128 characters (from 0 to 127), we set our first offset to 127 and then terminate our screen location at the offset plus our beginning location. Since we begin at 0 (I-1024), we will end at 127 because that is our offset. Secondly, we use an offset of 128 in line 50 to get the inverse characters we generated in our first set. That is because any character we POKE in from 0 to 127 has the inverse same character at a value of the first character plus 128. Thus, for any character we want to display in inverse, we simply add 128 to the original POKE value.

```
10  PRINT CHR$(147)
20  FOR I = 1024 TO (1024 + 127)
30  POKE I,(I-1024) : NEXT
32  FOR X = 55296 TO (55296 + 127)
34  POKE X,1 : NEXT
40  FOR I = 1424 TO (1424 + 127)
50  L = I-1424 : POKE I,L + 128 : NEXT
52  FOR X = 55696 TO (55696 + 127)
54  POKE X,1 : NEXT
60  FOR I = 1 TO 15 : PRINT : NEXT
```

You might wonder why line 60 was included. Take it out and see what happens. The reason for that is because the cursor follows the line numbers in the program and not the screen locations being POKEd. Therefore, you can POKE in a screen character from the HOME position on the screen, and even though the location will output a character to the bottom of the screen, the cursor will remain near the top. Try it and see.

In order to easily see what characters are produced with different values we POKE into screen locations, the following program allows you to INPUT a value and then displays the character on the screen for you. Of particular interest in this program are lines 50 and 60. Line 50 prints out a message and ends it with a blank instead of a semi-colon. However, when the program is RUN, the character output is right next to the end of the string we entered in line 50. The reason for that is we POKEd the output in a screen address right next to the end of our string. We could have placed a semi-colon, comma or blank at the end of line 50 and the output would have been in the same place. Try it and see.

```
10  PRINT CHR$(147); CHR$(5)
20  PRINT: PRINT : INPUT "ENTER A NUMBER FROM 0 TO
255->";X
30  IF X > 255 THEN 20
40  PRINT CHR$(19) : FOR I = 1 TO 11 : PRINT : NEXT
50  PRINT "THE CHARACTER FOR"; X ; "IS "
60  POKE (1504 + 25), X : POKE (55776 + 25),1
70  PRINT : PRINT CHR$(18); "HIT ANY KEY TO CONTINUE
OR 'Q' TO QUIT";
80  GET HK$ : IF HK$ = "" THEN 80
90  IF HK$ < > "Q" THEN 10
```

Accessing Machine Language Subroutines

The SYS command can be a useful tool in speeding up your programs. A SYS command "runs" a machine-level subroutine in your computer's ROMs or in memory. In the COMMODORE 64 PROGRAMMER'S REFERENCE GUIDE there is a listing of your computer's ROM. (Also in the October/November, 1982 issue of COMMODORE, a ROM listing can be found on pages 90-93.) Along the far left side are the starting addresses of the various subroutines which can be SYSed from your BASIC program. The problem is that the listing is in HEXADECIMAL and you have to make the SYS's with decimal values. There are programs and charts available for converting hexadecimal to decimal. However, for the beginner, it would probably be more confusing than enlightening to go into either the conversion process or explain the monitor listing. Instead, we will make a list of some handy SYS's, and when you are more advanced, you can see how these SYS's jumped to a machine-level subroutine.

CHART IT!

In addition to having labels stuck all over my computer, I have a number of charts. The nice thing about a chart is that it has everything from a single category together in one place. You should make or buy or somehow get your hands on charts which will summarize SYS's, POKEs, and other handy locations and addresses. Also, in several computer magazines you can find charts. Make copies of the charts and, using rubber cement, paste them to cardboard and keep them handy.

MINI SYS CHART

SYS 58692	Same as CLR/HOME
SYS 58726	Same as HOME
SYS 59903	Clears entire line of text
SYS 59062	Advance cursor
SYS 59626	Scrolls up a line
SYS 59137	Back to previous line

Try some of the above SYS's in your programs to see their effect. Here are some programs to play with SYS.

```
10 SYS 58692
20 FOR I = 1 TO 800 : PRINT "X"; : NEXT
30 REM SOMETHING TO FILL THE SCREEN
40 SYS 58726 : REM HOME CURSOR
50 FOR I = 1 TO 10 : PRINT : NEXT
```

```
10 SYS 58692
20 FOR I = 1 TO 200 : SYS 59062 : NEXT
30 PRINT "HOW'D I GET HERE?"
```

```
10 SYS 58692
20 FOR I = 1 TO 840 : PRINT "&";: NEXT
30 FOR SCROLL = 1 TO 12
40 FOR PAUSE = 1 TO 400 : NEXT PAUSE
50 SYS 59626 : REM SCROLL
60 NEXT SCROLL
```

A Lot Of Sound

Now that we have seen that besides simply POKEing numbers in empty memory locations, we can also POKE in values at special locations to get some immediate result, we are ready to take a look at the COMMODORE-64's fantastic music capabilities. Actually, we won't be dealing just with music, but just about any sound we want. However, like the rest of this book, we will keep it simple and provide programs and instruction on how to get started.

To begin with, when we start making sounds, we will be using a special chip in the COMMODORE-64. It's called a 6581 chip or SID SOUND SYNTHESIZER CHIP. Up to now we've been involved with the 6510 micro-processor chip - the heart of your machine. Basically, we will be POKEing in values to the 6581 and getting back sound through our TV set. So before we go any further, turn up the sound on your TV. (If you have hooked up a monitor without a speaker, these exercises will not work.) At first what we will be doing will look extremely complicated, but as we go on, it will become simpler since we will see that we can make certain settings and SAVE these settings to tape or diskette, and then enter notes or sounds with only a few numbers.

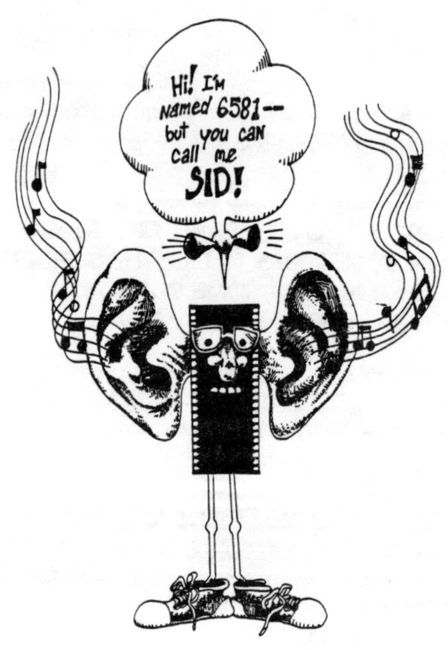

To begin let's take a look at the locations we will be POKEing and what they do.

> 1. VOLUME. This sets the volume of the output to a maximum of 15. Usually we will want to set the volume at this level when we are getting used to the sounds which can be produced. We will use the variable VL for volume.

> 2. ATTACK/DECAY and SUSTAIN/RELEASE. These two features refer to how fast a note rises to and then falls from its maximum volume level (attack/decay) and the rate to carry the note at a certain level before releasing it (sustain/release). We will use the variable AD for attack/decay and SR for sustain/release.

> 3. WAVEFORM. The waveform determines how sound will be produced. There are only 4 waveforms we will be using: Triangle = 17, Sawtooth = 33, Pulse = 65 and Noise = 129. We will use the variable WF for waveform.

> 4. HIGH/LOW FREQUENCY. These values make specific notes, each note requiring a single high and low frequency value. HF will denote high frequency and LF will denote low frequency.

As each of the above locations in the 6518 are POKEd, different sounds are emitted. For example, if we POKE VL,10 our volume value would be 10, and so we would have high/medium volume level. However, before we can POKE our variables, we have to define them first. So, let's start our program by defining the above variables. (Save the first part of the program on tape or disk as "SOUND VARIABLES" so that whenever you want to write a sound or music routine, you won't have to re-type all of the values.)

```
10  PRINT CHR$(147)
20  VL=54296:REM VOLUME LEVEL
30  LF=54272:REM LO-FREQUENCY VOICE1
40  HF=LF+1 :REM HI-FREQUENCY VOICE1
50  LW=LF+2 :REM LO-PULSE WIDTH VOICE1
60  HW=LF+3 :REM HI-PULSE WIDTH VOICE1
70  WF=LF+4 :REM WAVEFORM VOICE1
80  AD=LF+5 :REM ATTACK/DECAY VOICE1
90  SR=LF+6 :REM SUSTAIN/RELEASE VOICE1
```

Now that we have defined the variables to POKE, we will add the values to be POKEd in. In order to get a good idea of what is happening and the kind of results you will get with different values, we will make a series of INPUT statements so that you can easily test out different sounds and notes depending on what values you use.

```
100  PRINT:PRINT
110  INPUT "VOLUME (0-15)";V%
120  INPUT "ATTACK (0-15)";A%
130  INPUT "DECAY (0-15)";D%
140  INPUT "SUSTAIN (0-15)";S%
150  INPUT "RELEASE (0-15)";R%
160  INPUT "WAVEFORM (0-3)";W%: PRINT
165  IF W%<>2 THEN PRINT: GOTO 180
170  INPUT "PULSE WIDTH (0-20.47)";W1
180  INPUT "PITCH (.01-655.35)";P1
190  INPUT "DURATION(IN SECONDS)";DU
```

Now we have a routine for entering the values for the locations we will POKE. All that's left is to output the values and listen to our sounds!

```
200  W=16*2↑W%
205  W2%=W1/2.56: W3%=W1*100−W2%*256
210  P2%=P1/2.56: P3%=P1*100−P2%*256
215  POKE VL,V%
220  POKE AD,A%*16+D%
225  POKE SR,S%*16+R%
230  POKE WF,W+1
235  POKE LW,W3%: POKE HW,W2%+8
240  POKE LF,P3%: POKE HF,P2%
245  FOR T=1 TO 800*DU: NEXT
250  POKE WF,W
255  PRINT CHR$(19); "ANOTHER";
260  AN$="YES": INPUT AN$
265  IF LEFT$(AN$,1)="Y" THEN 100
300  PRINT CHR$(19);
310  POKE LF,0: POKE HF,0
320  END
```

Be sure the sound on your TV is turned up and RUN your program. Try all different kinds of combinations until you begin getting what you want.

Summary

This chapter has ventured into the COMMODORE-64's memory. While you are not expected to understand all of the nuances of our discussion, it is hoped that you have a general idea of how ASCII values work and a little about addresses and locations. Most important is that you have tried out some of the commands introduced and attempted to use them in your programs. The more you use different commands, the more you begin to understand what is happening.

The CHR$ function introduced ASCII values. Some of the uses of CHR$ allow us to access characters not available in our programming.

The POKE command enters a value to a decimal address and the PEEK command retrieves a value from an address. Special locations in your COMMODORE-64's memory have special functions, such as the ASCII screen values. More advanced uses of POKE and PEEK can provide a way of virtually writing machine-level subroutines.

CHAPTER 7

Using Graphics

Introduction

One of the nicest features of the COMMODORE-64 is its graphics capability. Basically, there are two kinds of graphics: (1) Screen Graphics and (2) Sprite Graphics. Screen graphics are something like text except that we use a lot more color and figures instead of letters and numbers. The way the graphics are used, however, we can access both graphics and text simultaneously. This feature is especially useful for labeling our graphics, such as charts or figures we may wish to create. As a matter of fact, if you have pressed the "Commodore key" and shift key and one of the other keys simultaneously, you may already have accessed some of your computer's graphics capabilities.

Sprite graphics are wholly different from screen graphics, and they are a good deal more difficult to use. However, sprite graphics give you an incredible amount of flexibility and power in creating figures in fine detail, especially animated ones for game applications. Once you become adept at using sprite graphics, there are limitless possibilities for the creation of colorful animated characters.

Screen Graphics

Screen graphics are very simple to use, since you can enter figures directly from the keyboard. To create a single figure you simply PRINT that figure in the same way you would a letter or number. For example, if you

PRINT "{SHIFT-Z}"

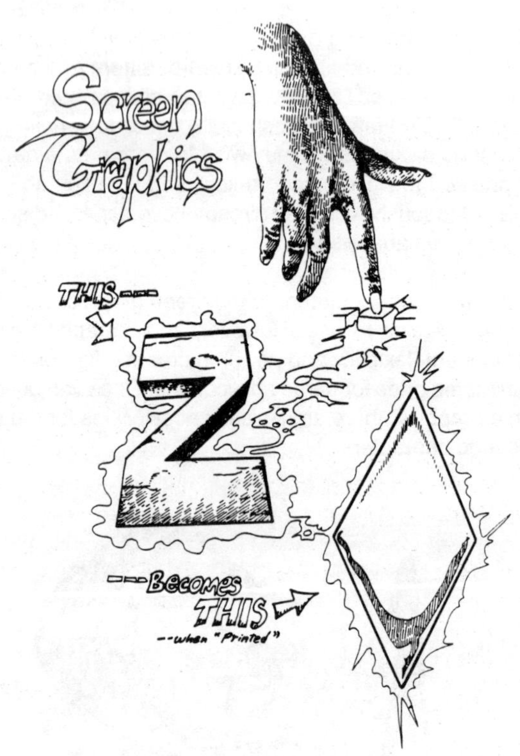

you will get a diamond figure. However, to create more interesting graphics, you will want to enter commands from the Program Mode. One way this can be done is by writing a series of PRINT statements, entering the drawing as you go along. For example, let's make a graphic playing card. We'll keep it simple and program a two of spades. (It would be a good idea to SAVE this program to disk or tape, as well as the others in this section. SAVE them under different file names since, even though some will have the identical results, they are programmed differently.)

```
10 PRINT CHR$(147)
20 PRINT "{SHIFT-U} {7 SHIFT-D's} {SHIFT-I}"
30 PRINT "{SHIFT-G} 2 {SHIFT-A} 5 SPACES {SHIFT-H}"
40 PRINT "{SHIFT-G} 7 SPACES {SHIFT-H}"
50 PRINT "{SHIFT-G} 3 SPACES {SHIFT-A} 3 SPACES {SHIFT-H}"
60 PRINT "{SHIFT-G} 7 SPACES {SHIFT-H}"
70 PRINT "{SHIFT-G} 3 SPACES {SHIFT-A} 3 SPACES {SHIFT-H}"
80 PRINT "{SHIFT-G} 7 SPACES {SHIFT-H}"
90 PRINT "{SHIFT-G} 5 SPACES 2 {SHIFT-A} {SHIFT-H}"
100 PRINT "{SHIFT-J} {7 SHIFT-F's} {SHIFT-K}"
```

When you are finished writing the program you should be able to see a "Two of Spades" on your screen - even before you RUN the program. When you do RUN it, the screen will clear and a "Two of Spades" will appear in the upper left hand corner of your TV. In the same way, you can draw anything else you want with the different shapes and characters on your keyboard. REMEMBER, to get the figure on the right side of the key, use the SHIFT key, and to print the characters on the left side of the key, use the COMMODORE key.

Let's take another look at our "Two of Spades" and see if we can improve the program. First, note that lines 40, 60 and 80 are identical, as are lines 50 and 70. Instead of having to re-write those lines, let's use our GOSUB commands, treating the repeated lines as subroutines. Using your editor, change line 40 to line 200 and line 50 to 300. Now add a colon and RETURN after lines 200 and 300. Then change lines 40, 60 and 80 to read GOSUB 200, and lines 50 and 70 to read GOSUB 300. Add line 110 END. The program should now look as follows:

```
10 PRINT CHR$(147)
20 PRINT "{SHIFT-U} {7 SHIFT-D's} {SHIFT-I}"
30 PRINT "{SHIFT-G} 2 {SHIFT-A} 5 SPACES {SHIFT-H}"
40 GOSUB 200
50 GOSUB 300
60 GOSUB 200
70 GOSUB 300
80 GOSUB 200
90 PRINT "{SHIFT-G} 5 SPACES 2 {SHIFT-A} {SHIFT-H}"
100 PRINT "{SHIFT-J} (7 SHIFT-F's) {SHIFT-K}"
110 END
200 PRINT "{SHIFT-G} 7 SPACES {SHIFT-H}" : RETURN
300 PRINT "{SHIFT-G} 3 SPACES {SHIFT-A} 3 SPACES {SHIFT-H}" : RETURN
```

Now that didn't save a lot of programming time, but if you begin to think of screen graphics as you would any other program, you will want to look for shortcuts to save both memory space and minimize programing redundancy. Now, to see how easy it is to change the two of spades to a three of hearts, using your editor, change the 2 of spades in lines 30 and 90 to a three of hearts - 3 (SHIFT-S), and the spade in line 300 to a heart. Now change line 60 from GOSUB 200 to GOSUB 300. This time when you RUN the program, you have an entirely different card and you made only a few changes. Try out different suits and see if you can make an entire deck.

EDIT IT!!

If you did not use your editor to change the above lines, you are working too hard! All that is required when you edit a line is to enter the changes and hit RETURN. To change a line to a different line number, simply enter the new line number over the old line number. For example, to change line 40 in our original "Two of Spades" to line 200, simply use the cursor key to walk up to line 40, place the cursor over the "4", enter "200" and press RETURN. When you LIST the program, line 40 will still be there in its original form, but there will now be a line 200 identical to line 40.

Coloring Your Graphics

If all of the graphics we did were in the two shades of blue on your screen, it would be pretty dull. However, if you do not have a color TV or monitor, the colors will appear as different shades of black and white or green (if you have a green screen monitor). The different color patterns will create different density in the lines and figures you create. If you have something other than a color TV or monitor, it is best to experiment with white (using CHR$(5) or CTRL-2) until you get used to the commands. Later when you get used to the line patterns created on a non-color screen, you can mix them for different effects.

Assuming you have a color screen, it might be necessary to adjust your TV/monitor to get the proper colors. One way we can do that is to make a color test chart program. The following program uses only half of your COMMODORE-64's range of colors, but that is because we can only access half using the keyboard or CHR$ commands. We'll get to the second half of your colors in a bit, but for now we'll make our color chart so that you can adjust your TV set. (Leave out the REM statements when you enter the program.)

```
10 PRINT CHR$ (147) : FOR V = 1 TO 7 : NEXT V : REM
CLEARS SCREEN AND TABS DOWN 7 PLACES
20 FOR I = 1 TO 8 : READ C(I) : NEXT : REM READS IN THE
CHR$ VALUES FOR THE COLORS IN DATA STATEMENT IN
LINE 100
30 FOR J = 1 TO 8
40 PRINT CHR$ (18); CHR$(C(J)); : FOR K = 1 TO 30 : PRINT
CHR$(32); : NEXT K : REM TURNS ON THE "COLOR ACCEP-
TOR" {CHR$(18)} AND THE NEXT COLOR AND THEN PRINTS
30 SPACES.
50 PRINT : NEXT J : PRINT CHR$(5)
60 PRINT SPC(10); "COLOR CHART"
100 DATA 5, 28, 30, 31, 144, 156, 158, 159 : REM THE CHR$
CODES FOR THE COLORS
```

Run the program and adjust your set. Once that's done, we can begin
doing more with different colors.

BACK TO NORMAL

Since we will be changing the screen to all kinds of colors, remember, to get it back to normal just press the RUN/STOP and RESTORE
keys simultaneously.

Let's go back to our "Two of Spades" program. Since spades are black,
let's turn our card from light blue to black. To do that, LOAD your "Two of
Spades" program into memory and add the following line:

```
15 PRINT CHR$(18); CHR$(144)
```

That was easy. Do the same with the "Three of Hearts" program, but
instead of using CHR$(144) use CHR$(28) for red. Play with the different
colors for a while to see what you get. The following chart shows the color
and its associated CHR$ value.

COLOR	CHR$ VALUE
White	5
Red	28
Green	30
Blue	31
Black	144
Purple	156
Yellow	158
Cyan	159

Now let's make a simple bar graph using a combination of screen graphics and a little text at the bottom of the screen.

```
10 PRINT CHR$(147)
20 INPUT "TITLE OF PLOT"; T$
30 PRINT : PRINT : INPUT "HOW MANY PLOTS (1-7)"; P% :
IF P% > 7 THEN 10
40 FOR C = 1 TO P% : READ C(C) : NEXT C
50 FOR I = 1 TO P%
60 PRINT "VALUE OF PLOT#" ; I ; : INPUT "(1-20)"; P(I) : IF
P(I) > 20 THEN 60
70 NEXT I
```

```
80 REM *** END INPUT BLOCK ***
100 PRINT CHR$ (147) : S=4
110 FOR I = 1 TO P%
120 PRINT CHR$(19)
130 FOR V = 0 TO (20 - P(I)) : PRINT : NEXT V
140 FOR PT = 1 TO P(I)
150 PRINT CHR$(18) ; CHR$(C(I)); SPC(S) ; CHR$(32) ; CHR$(32) : NEXT PT
160 PRINT CHR$(5) ; TAB(S) ; I : S=S+4
170 NEXT I : PRINT CHR$(28); : FOR LN = 1 TO 39 : PRINT CHR$(100); : NEXT LN
180 L = 20 - LEN(T$)/2 : PRINT CHR$(5); SPC(L); T$
190 GET A$ : IF A$ = "" THEN 190
200 REM *** END OUTPUT BLOCK ***
500 DATA 5, 28, 30, 144, 156, 158, 159 : REM CHR$ COLOR CODES EXCEPT FOR BLUE
```

RUN the program and see how nicely you can present data graphically. The program is severely limited in that it only does a maximum of 7 plots and values from 0 to 20. It is simple to change the number of plots above 7 - just change the trap value to a higher number, change the number of colors, change the offset (S variable) and make the bars narrower by using 1 CHR$(32) in line 150. Changing the values to above 20 requires more sophisticated manipulations, however. This is because 20 represents the maximum length of a vertical plot and still puts in the material at the bottom of the screen. Using a 2 bar plot, we will examine how to enter any range of numbers we want.

```
10 PRINT CHR$(147)
20 PRINT : PRINT : INPUT "MAX VALUE->";MV
30 N = 1:NN = MV : REM FOR MORE PRECISE CALCULA-
TIONS LET N = .1
40 IF NN > 20 THEN N = N + 1:NN = MV / N: GOTO 40
50 FOR I = 1 TO 2
60 PRINT "PLOT VALUE"; I; : INPUT PV(I)
70 PV(I) = INT (PV(I) / N)
80 NEXT I
90 REM *** END INPUT BLOCK ***
100 PRINT CHR$(147); : FOR PL = 1 TO 2
110 C$ = CHR$(32) + CHR$(32) + CHR$(32) + CHR$(32) :
REM MAKING BARS 4 SPACES WIDE
120 PRINT CHR$(19): FOR V=0 TO (20-PV(PL)) : PRINT: NEXT
130 FOR PT = 1 TO PV(PL) : PRINT CHR$(18); CHR$(28);
SPC(PL * 10); C$ : NEXT PT
```

```
140 NEXT PL
150 FOR LN = 1 TO 39 : PRINT CHR$(30); CHR$(100); : NEXT
160 PRINT CHR$ (5)
170 PRINT SPC(9); "PLOT 1"; SPC(5); "PLOT 2";
180 GET A$ : IF A$ = "" THEN 180
```

In order to understand what happened, we will go over the significant lines and explain each.

1. In line 30 the variable NN is defined to equal the maximum value (MV) entered in line 20.

2. In line 40, the crucial line for creating a proportional scale, NN is compared with 20 to find if the maximum value is greater than 20. If it is greater, then the counter variable N is incremented by 1 and NN is re-defined to be the value of MV divided by N and looped back to the beginning of the line for another comparison. As soon as the value of N increases to a point where the maximum value, MV, divided by N is not greater than 20, the loop exits. Whatever the value of N is at that time will be used in the rest of the program to divide any value entered.

FOR EXAMPLE:

The value of MV is established to be 100. Since 100 is greater than 20, 1 is added to N and 100 is divided by 2 resulting in the value of NN equaling 50. Since 50 is still larger than 20, N is incremented to 3. When MV is divided by 3, the result is 33.33. Again it is larger than 20, so there is another loop. The loop repeats until N is equal to 5. Now MV divided by N equals 20. This time, when the comparison to 20 is made, it is found that NN is not larger than 20 and so the line is exited and the value of N is established at 5. No matter what value is entered, as long as it does not exceed the maximum value, there will be no errors since all plot values PV (1), etc., will be divided by 5. Since 100 is the maximum value to be entered, 20 is the maximum value that will be charted.

3. Two values for PV (I) are entered in line 60, and in line 70 PV(I) is divided by N. The INT command is introduced to provide an integer (whole) number for charting.

4. In line 110, C$ is defined as the concatenation of 4 spaces, CHR$(32). This is to make our graph bars 4 spaces wide.

5. Lines 120 through 140 chart our plots, very much like what was done in our first chart program.

FOR THE PERFECTIONIST WITH SOME TIME

We incremented N by 1 each time we passed through our test loop in line 40. If we wanted to get a finer value, we could have incremented N by .1 or .01 or even .00001! This would give us a nearer minimum value by which to divide PV(I) and still keep it proportional. However, it would take longer for the loop to find the minimum value of N. Change the program to see the different results in the charts. The smaller the increment, the closer to the top of the chart the maximum value will appear, but the longer the program will take to execute.

We have spent a good deal of time working on charts in screen graphics, but it is important to see the practical applications of such graphics. Often users simply see screen graphics as something to draw mosaic pictures on and nothing else; but, as we have seen, it is possible to make very good practical use of them as well. Now let's have a little fun with animation before going on to POKEing graphics in the screen.

Animation in screen graphics can be used in games and for special effects. However, we will only touch upon some elementary examples to provide you with the concepts of how animation works. Basically, by placing a figure on the screen, covering it up and then putting it in a new position, you can create the illusion of moving figures. It works in exactly the same way as animated cartoons. A series of frames are flashed on the screen sequentially. Even though each individual frame has a stationary figure, by rapidly flashing a series of such frames, the figures appear to move. You computer does the same thing. For example, the following little program appears to bounce a ball in the upper left hand corner:

```
10 PRINT CHR$(147)
20 PRINT "{SHIFT-Q} " : REM SPACE BETWEEN SHIFT-Q AND
SECOND QUOTATION MARK
30 FOR I = 1 TO 100 : NEXT
40 PRINT CHR$ (19) : PRINT " {SHIFT-Q}" : REM SPACE
BETWEEN FIRST QUOTATION MARK AND SHIFT-Q
50 FOR I = 1 TO 100 : NEXT
60 PRINT CHR$(19) : GOTO 20
```

What appeared to be a moving "ball," was actually a figure being placed on the screen, erased, and then replaced in a different location. Now let's do the same thing on the vertical axis and use cursor movement within our program. Also, just for fun, let's add some sound and special effects.

```
10 PRINT CHR$(147) : REM *** BEGIN ANIMATION BLOCK ***
20 FOR I = 1 TO 25
30 PRINT TAB(20); "{SHIFT-Q} {UP-CURSOR}" : REM A WHITE
AND INVERSE BALL WILL APPEAR ON YOUR SCREEN
40 FOR J = 1 TO 50 : NEXT J : REM DELAY LOOP TO SLOW
MOVEMENT
50 PRINT TAB(20); "{SPACE}" : REM PUTS SPACE WHERE
BALL WAS
60 PRINT : REM FORCE DISPLAY DOWN ONE LINE
70 NEXT I
80 GOSUB 200
90 PRINT TAB(20); "*" : REM *** END ANIMATION BLOCK ***
100 GET A$ : IF A$ = "" THEN 100
110 END
200 REM *** SOUND EFFECTS ***
210 POKE 54296,15 : POKE 54277,20 : POKE 54278,60 : REM
SET VOLUME, ATTACK/DECAY AND SUSTAIN/RELEASE
220 POKE 54273,5 : POKE 54272,185 : POKE 54276,129 : REM
SET HIGH/LOW FREQUENCY AND WAVEFORM
```

230 FOR DU = 1 TO 50 : NEXT DU : REM SET DURATION
240 POKE 54277,0 : POKE 54278,0 : POKE 54276,0 : RETURN
: REM TURN OFF SOUND AND RETURN

By experimenting with different algorithms, you can create a wide range
of effects. If you have played arcade games with movement and sound,
you now have an idea of how they were created. Now, go ahead and start
working on that SUPER SPACE BLASTER ALIEN EATER game.

Now that we have an idea about how we can make things move, let's do
some more work with color. First, we will see how to change the background color and border of our screen, and then we will examine the
screen and color memory maps in the COMMODORE-64 to put anything
anywhere in any color on our screen.

To begin, let's go back to our "Two of Spades" program. Now we already
noted that the card should be black instead of light blue, but every card
player also knows that "green felt" is the correct background for the "table."
To change the background and border colors, we use the following POKES:

        POKE 53281, (0-15) Background Color
        POKE 53280, (0-15) Border Color

Load your "Two of Spades" into memory, press CTRL-1 to change the
drawing color to black, and now POKE 53281,5. When you RUN the
program now, you will have a black card on a green background. Since
the borders of card tables are made of wood, let's change the border to
brown with a POKE 53280,9. There's our black two of spades on what
looks more like a card table! (To get everything back to normal, remember
to just press RUN/STOP and RESTORE.)

It is quite simple to change the colors of the background and borders. The
following are the color codes for the 16 colors you can access.

0 BLACK	4 PURPLE	8 ORANGE	12 GRAY 2
1 WHITE	5 GREEN	9 BROWN	13 LIGHT GREEN
2 RED	6 BLUE	10 LIGHT RED	14 LIGHT BLUE
3 CYAN	7 YELLOW	11 GRAY 1	15 GRAY 3

To get used to what's available, the following program gives you a quick
trip through the various background and border colors.

```
10 PRINT CHR$(147)
20 BG = 53281 : BD = 53280
30 INPUT "BACKGROUND COLOR "; B1 : IF B1 > 15 THEN
30
40 INPUT "BORDER COLOR"; B2 : IF B2 > 15 THEN 40
50 POKE BG,B1 : POKE BD,B2
60 GOTO 10
```

When you RUN the program, experiment with different text colors as well by pressing CTRL and keys 1 through 8. You will find that certain text colors are more or less clear with certain background colors. (White on white is *very* difficult to read!)

You may have noticed that we were able to change the border and background colors to 16 different hues, but we still can get only 8 colors for our keyboard characters. To access all colors for our keyboard characters, we will have to understand the COMMODORE-64's screen and color memory maps. As you know, your screen is a 40 by 25 matrix. Each element of the matrix is represented by an address in your computer's memory. Your screen's memory map begins at 1024 and ends at 2023, giving you 1000 locations to put something on the screen. By POKEing these locations with different values, you are able to place characters on the screen anywhere you want. Each character has a code, very much like CHR$ codes, except the code numbers are different, and rather than PRINTing them, you POKE them. For example, the code for the letter "A" is 1. If you POKE a location between 1024 and 2023 with "1" an "A" will appear there. For example, clear your screen and POKE 1475,1. In the middle of your screen, a white "A" appears. But note the location of your cursor. It is still near the top of your screen. That is because you did not PRINT the letter at the location of the cursor, but instead you accessed a memory location. To watch these memory locations fill up with "A's" enter the following from the Immediate Mode:

```
FOR I = 1024 TO 2023 : POKE I, 1 : NEXT
```

Now to see the different codes, key in the following little program which will give you a run-through of the codes in the middle of your screen:

```
10 PRINT CHR$(147)
20 FOR I = 0 TO 127
30 POKE 1484, I
40 FOR J = 1 TO 200 : NEXT J : NEXT I
```

Now let's take an animated tour of our screen. We'll start with location 1024 and travel with an arrow (code 62) to location 2023.

```
10 PRINT CHR$(147)
20 BG = 1024 : ES = 2023
30 FOR I = BG TO ES : POKE I, 62 : FOR J = 1 TO 5 : NEXT
J : POKE I, 96
40 FOR K = 1 TO 5 : NEXT K : NEXT I
```

To create animation on our screen, we first POKEd an arrow, gave it a
short delay, then POKEd a space (code 96) in the same location, gave it
a short delay, and then went on to the next memory location. Using memory screen locations, we have far more power over characters and animation, for we can go from any point to another without having to worry
where the cursor is. Let's go back to our bouncing ball, but this time do it
with POKEs.

```
10 PRINT CHR$(147)
20 FOR I = (1024 + 20) TO 1984 STEP 40
30 POKE I,81 : FOR D = 1 TO 10 : NEXT D
40 POKE I,96 : FOR X = 1 TO 10 : NEXT X : NEXT I
50 FOR I = (1984 + 20) TO 1024 STEP -40
60 POKE I,81 : FOR D = 1 TO 10 : NEXT D
70 POKE I,96 : FOR X = 1 TO 10 : NEXT X : NEXT I
80 GOTO 20
```

Note that we started with the top left corner and added an offset of "20"
to put the ball into the middle of the screen. Then we reversed the process
in line 50 .

Now let's look at the color memory map. It begins at location 55296 and
ends at location 56295. Again, it is 1000 locations, and think of it as an
overlay on your screen map. The upper left hand corner of your screen
map is 1024 and on your color map it is 55296. First, we will POKE in a
character on your screen map and then a color for that character on your
color map.

```
POKE 1024,81 <RETURN>
POKE 55296,8 <RETURN>
```

First the ball appeared and then it was colored orange, a color you did
not have for your characters before now.

Now at this juncture you may be asking yourself, "How in the world am I
expected to figure out one of a thousand screen locations, then one of
127 character codes and then superimpose a thousand different color

map locations with one of 16 colors on top of the screen map and get it in the correct place?" Actually, it is not as difficult as it sounds, and like everything else having to do with such calculations, let your computer do the work! The following is a step-by-step outline of how to set up a program to do your calculations using variables.

BS = 1024 <-Beginning location of your screen map.

BC = 55296 <-Beginning location of your color map.

CS = XXXX <-Current location (with XXXX being a number from1024 to 2023) of your character on the screen.

OF = CS - BS <-Your offset based on the difference between your current location and the starting location on the screen map.

CC = BC + OF <-Color map location to place color.

C1 = XX <-Character code for screen character with XX being a value from 0 to 127.

C2 = XX <-Color code with XX being a value from 0 to 15.

Essentially, the way to determine the mutual location for the screen and color map is to have your computer count the number of locations between the beginning of the map and the current location. Since both maps use sequential addresses, the same offset can be used for both maps. The following program uses the above variables and allows you to place characters anywhere you want them.

```
10 PRINT CHR$(147)
20 BS = 1024 : BC = 55296
30 INPUT "SCREEN LOCATION (1024-2023)" ;CS
40 INPUT "CHARACTER CODE (0-127)"; C1
50 OF = CS - BS : CC = BC + OF
60 INPUT "COLOR CODE (0-15)"; C2
70 POKE CS,C1 : POKE CC,C2
80 GET A$ : IF A$ = "" THEN 80
90 GOTO 10
```

Play with the program until you get used to the idea of what codes give you different characters and colors in various locations. Once you're finished, try the following program to give you a "Beaded Curtain" and show another way to create effects with color using programmed POKEs.

```
10 PRINT CHR$(147)
20 BS = 1024 : ES = 2023 : REM BEGINNING AND ENDING
ADDRESSES OF SCREEN MAP
30 BC = 55296 : EC = 56295
40 FOR I = BS TO ES : POKE I, 81 : NEXT I
50 FOR C = BC TO EC STEP 2 : POKE C,8 : NEXT C
60 FOR NC = (BC + 1) TO EC STEP 2 : POKE NC,4 : NEXT
70 FOR C = BC TO EC STEP 2 : POKE C,5 : NEXT C
80 FOR NC = (BC + 1) TO EC STEP 2 : POKE NC,6 : NEXT
90 GET S$ : IF S$ = "" THEN 90
100 PRINT CHR$(147)
```

Suppose you don't want to have to look up every character you key in.
Let's say you want to write your name or a chart heading or anything else
simply by using an INPUT statement and the keyboard. Well, you can use
the screen map and POKE in characters. To do this, we will have to learn
a new command, ASC. The ASC command converts the first character of
a string to a CHR$ code. For example, the ASCII code for an "A" is 65. If
you keyed in

```
PRINT ASC("A")
```

you would get

```
65
```

Now, since the CHR$ values won't do you any good for POKEs, we will
have to convert the CHR$ value to a POKE value. If you look at your
screen display codes and ASCII and CHR$ codes, you will see that the
ASCII alphabet begins at 65 and the screen codes at 1. To convert one
to the other, we simply add or subtract 64, depending on which way we
want to convert. Since we want to convert ASCII into screen codes, we
will subtract 64 from whatever ASC value we determine. For example, key
in the following:

```
10 PRINT CHR$(147)
20 INPUT "ENTER LETTER FROM A-Z: "; A$
30 A = ASC(A$) : A1 = A-64
40 POKE 1024,A1
50 GOTO 20
```

As you saw, every time you keyed in a letter, that letter would appear in
white in the upper left hand corner of your screen (location 1024).

Now that we know how to get a single letter in a single location, let's see if we can get entire strings on the screen. To do this, we must do the following:

1. Define or INPUT our string

2. Break up our string into individual letters so that we can get the ASCII values for each character. (The ASC command reads only the left-most character of a string.)

3. Convert the ASCII values into screen display codes.

4. POKE in the codes.

Using our offset of 64, this means that we will have to use our MID$ command to examine each character. However, when we come to a space (ASCII value 32), we will run into trouble since 32 - 64 is a negative number. To fix that, we'll set a trap for spaces and define them with the correct POKE value - which also just happens to be 32! To keep things simple, we'll use the upper left hand corner of our screen to print our strings.

```
10 PRINT CHR$(147)
20 PRINT : PRINT : INPUT "YOUR NAME:"; NA$
30 BS = 1024 : BC = 55296
40 DIM A (LEN(NA$)) , A1(LEN(NA$)) : REM DIMENSION OUR
ARRAYS IN CASE THE NAME IS LONGER THAN 11
50 FOR I = 1 TO LEN (NA$)
55 IF ASC(MID$(NA$,I,1)) = 32 THEN A1(I) = 32 : NEXT I :
REM TRAP FOR SPACES
60 A(I) = ASC(MID$(NA$,I,1)) : A1(I) = A(I) - 64 : REM CON-
VERT FROM ASCII TO SCREEN CODE
70 NEXT I
80 FOR P = 1 TO LEN(NA$) : POKE BS + P, A1(P) : NEXT P
: REM POKE IN THE CODE
100 REM *** CHART COLOR ***
110 INPUT "COLOR CODE (0-15)"; C2
120 FOR C = 1 TO LEN(NA$) : POKE BC + C,C2 : NEXT C
130 GET W$ : IF W$ = "" THEN 130
140 RUN
```

Now if you entered a period (.), you got an ILLEGAL QUANTITY ERROR IN 60. This is because the period, like the space, has an ASCII value of less than 65. If you want to fix the program to accept periods, take a look at line 55 where we trapped spaces. Try entering a similar trap for periods in line 56 so that you can enter periods without getting an error. Otherwise, you should now be able to see how to POKE characters in from the keyboard and write programs using strings to be POKEd in the screen map.

Sprite Graphics

Now that we have an idea of how to go about using graphics on the 40 by 25 screen, let's take a look at a very powerful aspect of your COM-MODORE-64, sprite graphics. First off, we'll have to explain what "sprites" are and what you may want to use them for. Essentially, a sprite is a figure in memory. Depending on what you place in special memory locations, you will get different figures or "sprites." They can be used in animation and game development, but they also may be used to liven up virtually any presentation.

The good news about sprites in your COMMODORE-64 is that you have a tremendous amount of control in their creation since you enter them in a translated binary code. The "bad" news is that they are a bit tricky to understand. However, if we organize ourselves into the basic components of programming sprites, the effort will be worth the trouble. To pique your interest let's start with a simple example. Key in the following, and you will get a little "Sprite Space Fighter." We'll explain what happened later on, but for now, key in the program and watch what happens.

```
10 PRINT CHR$(147)
20 BG = 53248 : REM BEGIN GRAPHICS CHIP
30 TU = BG + 21 : REM TURN ON ADDRESS FOR SPRITE
"XX"
40 S1 = 2 : REM VALUE OF SPRITE 1
50 L = 2040 : REM BEGINNING LOCATION OF SPRITE
POINTER
60 SS = 832 : REM START OF STORAGE LOCATION FOR
SPRITE DATA
70 SL = 13 : REM BLOCK WHERE DATA STORED (13TH
BLOCK)
80 X1 = BG + 2 : Y1 = BG + 3 : REM X,Y MOVE ADDRESSES
90 REM *** END VARIABLE DEFINITION BLOCK ***
200 FOR R = 0 TO 29 : READ D : POKE SS + R, D : NEXT R
: REM READ IN DATA TO CONSTRUCT SPRITE FROM LINES
500-520
210 POKE TU, S1 : REM TURN ON SPRITE #1
220 POKE L + 1 , SL : REM READ IN SPRITE DATA FOR
SPRITE #1
230 POKE Y1, 100 : REM VERTICAL LOCATION AT 100
240 FOR H = 0 TO 255
250 POKE X1, H : NEXT H : REM HORIZONTAL LOCATION
260 GOTO 240 : REM CONTINUOUS LOOP
270 REM **** END SPRITE CREATION AND MOVEMENT BLOCK
****

500 DATA 2, 0, 64, 2, 0, 64, 2, 24, 64
510 DATA 2, 60, 64, 2, 102, 64, 3, 255, 192
520 DATA 2, 60, 64, 2, 24, 64, 2, 0, 64, 2, 0, 64
```

Now if everything is done correctly, you should see a little "space fighter" move horizontally across your screen. There's a lot more you can do with sprites, but let's use the above example to explain what is happening.

The first concept to examine is that of binary arithmetic. If we conceive of our sprites as little dots on the screen which are together in blocks, we can understand both binary math and sprites. To begin, we will examine

an 8 bit byte, numbered from 7 to 0, each containing a 0 or 1 - the only
two numbers in the binary system.

7	6	5	4	3	2	1	0
0	1	0	1	1	0	1	0

For your computer to do math, it must convert everything into the binary
system, and the 6510 microprocessor in your COMMODORE-64 does
this in chunks called "bytes" 8 "bits" long. The above binary number
"01011010" is translated into the decimal number "90", and whenever you
key in "90", your computer translates it into "01011010".

It makes this conversion automatically, but in order to make sprites, it will
be necessary for you to do it. However, it is really quite simple. In binary
arithmetic, since we have only 2 digits, whenever we run out of unique
combinations, we tack on a 0 to the end and start over again. We do the
same in decimal math. For example, when we get to 9 in decimal, we start
over with a "1" and tack on a "0" to get 10. Counting in binary, we have
the following:

```
   0 = 0
   1 = 1
  10 = 2
  11 = 3
 100 = 4
 101 = 5
 110 = 6
 111 = 7
1000 = 8
```

It is just like when we reach 9, 99, or 999, we start over with 1 and add
another digit. In binary, we start over with 11, 111, 1111, etc. since we
have only 0 and 1 to work with. However, because we are not used to
working in a binary system, we have to have a simple way to convert
binary to decimal. In your COMMODORE-64 manual on page 78 there is
an excellent little program to convert binary into decimal, and I strongly
recommend you use it to make your conversion when you start making
sprites. (However, add the following line for a smooth exit: 11 IF A$ =
"X" THEN END : REM EXIT PROGRAM BY ENTERING X.)

Another simple way of making conversions is to remember that each bit
has a different value whether there is a 0 or 1 in the bit. Let's look at these
values and how they can be used for conversion:

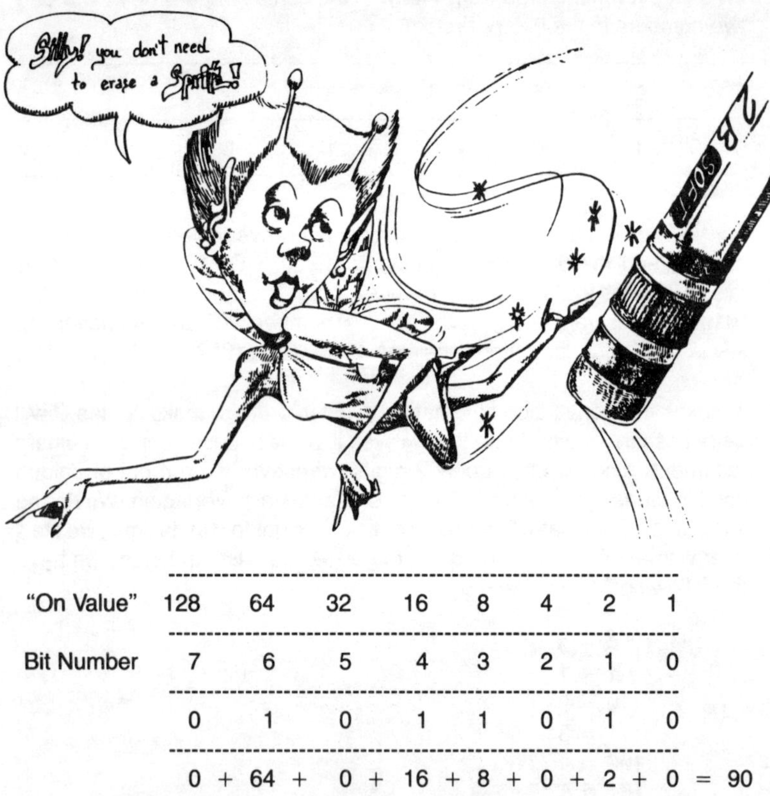

"On Value"	128	64	32	16	8	4	2	1
Bit Number	7	6	5	4	3	2	1	0
	0	1	0	1	1	0	1	0

0 + 64 + 0 + 16 + 8 + 0 + 2 + 0 = 90

To get our decimal value, just add the sum of the "on values" together.

Now the obvious question is "Why bother?" Well, since sprites are made up of little dots or "pixels" which are created by the various bits being "on", we can create any shapes we want by turning on the combination of bits we want. Then by converting the binary patterns to decimal we can POKE in the bit patterns from BASIC. To begin, let's see how our "space fighter" in the above program was created. Here's what you'll need:

1. Some graph paper.
2. A pencil and clean eraser
3. A ruler

On the graph paper, draw a 24 wide by 21 long matrix. Divide the matrix vertically into 3 parts. Each part will be 8 squares wide and 21 deep. Each row has 3 parts, each made of 8 squares. The 3 parts represent 3 bytes, just as in our figure above. Since we have 21 rows and 3 bytes in each row, we have a total of 21 x 3 or 63 bytes in our "block." Each block represents 1 sprite. We don't have to use the entire block, but we must think of our sprites in terms of these blocks. We will read our rows from left to right, stopping at each new byte. If you use the binary conversion program from your COMMODORE-64 manual, enter the numbers from the leftmost "square" or "bit" to the rightmost square in the byte. DO NOT MIX BYTES.

Let's take a look at the following figure and see how the sprite data is created.

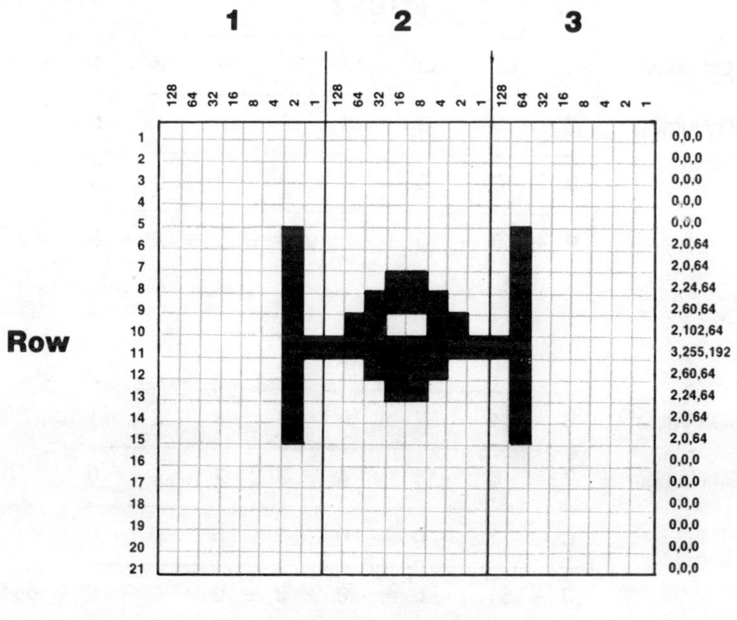

"Sprite Fighter"

In our sprite, we did not enter any information until Row 6. We could enter DATA 0,0,0 for Rows 1-5, but unless we want our sprite in the middle of the block in memory, there is no reason to do so. (In some applications there *is* reason to do so!) Likewise, we had no information in the last 6 rows, and we can leave them blank or enter 0's. In applications where you use several sprites in the same memory locations, you will want to fill the block to erase any unwanted pixels when you want one figure replaced by another. Let's look at a row and see how we converted a piece of our drawing.

BYTE #1

	128	64	32	16	8	4	2	1
"On Value"	128	64	32	16	8	4	2	1
Bit Number	7	6	5	4	3	2	1	0
	0	0	0	0	0	0	1	0

0 + 0 + 0 + 0 + 0 + 0 + 2 + 0 = 2

BYTE #2

	128	64	32	16	8	4	2	1
"On Value"	128	64	32	16	8	4	2	1
Bit Number	7	6	5	4	3	2	1	0
	0	0	0	0	0	0	0	0

0 + 0 + 0 + 0 + 0 + 0 + 2 + 0 = 0

BYTE #3

	128	64	32	16	8	4	2	1
"On Value"	128	64	32	16	8	4	2	1
Bit Number	7	6	5	4	3	2	1	0
	0	1	0	0	0	0	0	0

0 + 64 + 0 + 0 + 0 + 0 + 0 + 0 = 64

Now, while the process is admittedly somewhat involved and exacting, it is more a matter of organization than complexity. After all, it is relatively simple to draw a sprite on graph paper once you have your plot set up, and since you can draw fairly detailed shapes your efforts are rewarded. Also, if you draw sprites like the one in the example, certain rows repeat themselves; so once you have figured out the values for a row, all you have to do when they are repeated is to enter the identical data.

Now that we see how to create sprites, the next step is to get them to do tricks for us. First of all, we have to be aware of the layout of the area through which we move. Basically, it is a 320 by 200 matrix. We can move 320 dots or pixels horizontally and 200 vertically. However, your sprite is 24 pixels across and 21 down. When it is drawn, it will appear to "enter" the side of the screen a part at a time, as though it is moving as a whole from somewhere in your TV set. For moving it, though, think of your screen as a football field, 320 yards by 200 yards, and the "play" is the X,Y coordinates on that field. Location 160,100 would put you right in the middle. Increasing the X value moves you to the right and increasing the Y value moves you down.

Before we get to movement, first we have to get the sprite data into memory and turn on the graphics and sprite. In our sample program we used the variable BG for the beginning location of graphics, "Begin Graphics." (BG = 53248). Most of the other needed locations are an offset of BG; so as we define more variables, we incorporate BG along with the necessary offset. The following variables will be used:

BG = 53248 <-Begin graphics
TU = BG + 21 <- Make a given sprite appear or disappear.
TU stands for "Turn On" a given sprite or set of sprites.
S1 = 2 <- Value of sprite #1. Sprite values are:

S0 = 1
S1 = 2
S2 = 4
S3 = 8
S4 = 16

S5 = 32
S6 = 64
S7 = 128

L = 2040 <- Beginning of data handling. Offset of sprite by sprite number, not sprite value. For example, Sprite 0 = 0, Sprite 1 = 1, Sprite 2 = 2, etc. Uses 2040 to 2047 for storing data pointers, not actual data. SS = 832 <- Beginning of Sprite Storage. This is where the actual data are stored. Three groupings of data storage 832, 896 (832 + 64), and 960 (895 + 64) can be used. They must be kept separate and not overlap unless you want to create double or triple sized sprites. We only used the first one.

SL = 13 <- Storage "block" (832/63) for beginning at 832. For sprites stored at beginning location 895 SL = 14, for 958 SL = 15.

X1 = BG + 2 : Y1 = BG + 3 <- The X and Y coordinates for Sprite #1. All X and Y values are paired, beginning with 0,1 for Sprite 0, 2,3 for Sprite 1, 4,5 for Sprite 2, etc.

Now that we see what our variables mean, let's go through the program step by step beginning with line 200 to see what we did to make everything work:

FOR R = 0 TO 29 : READ D : POKE SS + R,D : NEXT R. Here we read in our data from lines 500 - 520 and stored it in sequential locations beginning at 832 (SS + 0).

POKE TU, S1. This turned on sprite 1.

POKE L + 1, SL This indicated that the data should be for sprite #1 found in block SL.

POKE Y1, 100. The Y or vertical location should be at 100, about the middle of the screen.

FOR H = 0 TO 255

POKE X1, H : NEXT H This moved the sprite from the horizontal location 0 to 255. The vertical location remained at 100, giving us horizontal movement only.

If you do not understand everything at this point, don't feel bad. The important points are not why information is stored at certain locations instead of others or why "blocks" are POKEd. Look at the sequence of commands, and see what happens if you make changes in the values. For example, if you wanted to turn on Sprite #3 instead of #1, what values would you have to change? If you wanted your sprite to move vertically instead of horizontally or zig zag, how could that be done? Well, the way to find out is to enter changes and review the above material until your sprites behave as you expect.

Color, Expansion and Full Horizontal Control With Sprites

Now that we understand something about creating and moving sprites, let's see how to change their color, expand them and get them to move all the way across the screen. Taking our example program, we will expand both the vertical and horizontal axes of our sprite. We will use the following variables:

    EX = BG + 29 <- Address of X axis expansion
    EY = BG + 23 <- Address of Y axis expansion

Add the following to your program:

    85 EX = BG + 29 : EY = BG + 23
    225 POKE EX,S1 : POKE POKE EY,S1

Now when you RUN the program, your sprite runs across the screen in a larger size. You want to change the color? OK, let's add some more variables:

    C = BG + 39 <- Beginning of color address.
    C1 = C + 1 <- Color address for Sprite #1. Use sprite number as offset (0 to 7).
    POKE C1, 2 <- Color red (2) selected. Use colors 0 - 15.

To get your colors in the program add the following lines:

    87 C = BG + 39 : C1 = C + 1
    227 POKE C1,2

Now you should have a big red "Sprite Fighter" moving across your screen. Change the colors by entering different values to be POKEd into C1 in line 227.

The next step is to get our sprite to move all the way across the screen. This involves "turning on" the "most significant byte" or MSB. However, rather than worrying about what an "MSB" is, think of it as a "screen extender" or the "rightmost screen movement." We will first turn it on, move our sprite, then turn it off and go back to our original movement. The results will be a continuously moving sprite across the full length of the screen.

```
RS = BG + 16 <- Right screen address.
```

Now, we will move the last 64 dots to the right side of the screen using a loop from 0 to 63. Add the following lines:

```
88 RS = BG + 16
252 POKE RS, S1
254 FOR HH = 0 TO 63 : POKE X1, HH : NEXT HH
256 POKE RS, 0
```

Now that we have seen the bag of tricks we can do with our sprites, let's add another sprite to our program. We will move both sprites independently of one another, color them different colors and have them in different sizes. First we have to draw another sprite. By sheer coincidence, I just happen to have another "Space Sprite" on hand. First add the following DATA lines for our new sprite:

```
600 DATA 0, 8, 0, 0, 28, 0, 3, 255, 224, 6, 127, 48, 12, 62, 24
610 DATA 24, 28, 12, 112, 8, 7
```

We will now create our second sprite using Sprite #4. Add (or change) the following lines in your program:

```
40 S1 = 2 : S4 = 16
80 X1 = BG + 2 : Y1 = BG + 3 : X4 = BG + 8 : Y4 = BG
+ 9
87 C = BG + 39 : C1 = C + 1 : C4 = C + 4
205 FOR R = 0 TO 20 : READ D: POKE (SS + 64) + R, D :
NEXT R
210 POKE TU, S1 + S4
220 POKE L + 1, SL : POKE L + 4, SL + 1
227 POKE C1, 13 : POKE C4, 10
245 POKE X4, H : POKE Y4, H
```

That's all there is to it. Now to see what we've done, line by line.

> Line 40: We added the value of Sprite #4 which is 16
> Line 80: The X and Y values of Sprite #4 are added.
> Line 87: The color address for Sprite #4 is defined.
> Line 205: We read in the data for our second sprite and, using an offset of 64, stored the data in block #14.
> Line 210: We turned on both Sprite #1 and Sprite #4. Note that this was done by *adding* the values of the two sprites rather than making two separate POKEs.
> Line 220. The offset for the address pointer was POKEd in for the second sprite and we indicated that it could be found in the next block, SL + 1.
> Line 227: We added color to Sprite #4 - Color #10, light red.
> Line 245: The X and Y locations for Sprite #4 were added.

That's about it for sprites, and whatever you want to do with them is left to your imagination. They are a bit more complicated than what we have dealt with previously, but if you remember to organize your programs into blocks, have recognizable variables and pay attention to the sequence, there is a great deal you can do with sprites. You may have noticed that animation is actually simpler with sprites than with previous animation we studied. We did not have to follow our sprites with an "erase," and you might notice that one sprite can pass "behind" another. So, while there is a good deal of figuring to be done, there is more you can create with sprites than with other forms of animation.

Summary

This chapter has taken us into the world of computer graphics. Beginning with screen graphics, we saw how we could mix graphics and text together to create graphs. Then we saw how we could animate screen figures by putting them in different screen locations, erasing them and then re-entering them at another location. We also found out how to color our graphics both from the keyboard and from POKEing the color screen on top of the figures we had entered. By programming with "offsets" we were able to coordinate our figures and colors.

The final part of our exploration into graphics took us into the world of sprites. Beginning with a drawing on graph paper, we transferred our creations to the computer's memory by translating our figures into binary images. Then we learned how to store the information into memory and bring out an animated sprite. Next, we added color and expanded both the size of our sprites and their placement on the screen. Finally, we saw how to create and animate multiple sprites simultaneously.

As a final note on graphics, it should be pointed out that besides being fun and artistic, computer graphics can be put to other practical uses as well. We saw, for example, how to create graphs with screen graphics, but you can also use sprite graphics in programs to make them clearer and more interesting. We naturally think of games when working with sprites and animation, but do not limit your use of graphics to the obvious. See how they can be employed to enhance information for your computer or used in some other creative manner.

CHAPTER 8

Data And Text Files With The Tape And Disk System

Introduction

In this chapter we are going to learn more about some advanced applications with the tape and disk system. We will be covering two types of files: (1) Data files and (2) Sequential Text Files. There are many similarities between data and sequential text files. Your disk system's data files are a type of sequential file, and we might even consider the way in which your cassette stores data to be a form of sequential text file. However, for the sake of clarity we will discuss each separately.

Before beginning, I want to point out that the COMMODORE floppy disk system is a very sophisticated and smart device. For beginners, it can be difficult to understand some of its more advanced applications, and there is a very real risk of destroying programs and data on your disk. Therefore, in this section, we will take each step slowly, and even at the risk of redundancy, explain the various functions of commands dealing with your disk system. Also, we will *not* be dealing with the most advanced features of the disk operating system, for they are beyond the scope of this book. However, we will be going to a "middle" range of sophistication, and it is strongly advised for those of you with a disk system to use a blank formatted disk on which you have *not* accumulated programs. By doing so you will not inadvertently destroy valuable data and programs. (This comes from the voice of experience, having clobbered numerous disks myself!)

Data Files and Your Cassette

Wouldn't it be nice if, after keying in a lot of data, you could save it to your tape? For example, let's say you have created a really nice sprite which takes up 21 rows of a sprite matrix, and you want to use that sprite in a different program than the one for which you originally developed it. Instead of having to re-enter all the sprite data, you could just load the the data into any program you wanted. Well, using data files, you can do that and a lot more. You can save any kind of data, numeric or string, to tape and then using a special set of commands we will learn, load that data directly into your program. You can create a check book program which saves all of your check entries tend balances to tape, make a mailing list that creates, saves and retrieves names, addresses and telephone numbers, or even a list of your favorite recipes.

In Chapters 1 and 2 we discussed how to SAVE a program and retrieve it with LOAD on your COMMODORE-64 using the Commodore C2N Cassette Unit. Both of these commands are executed in the Immediate Mode. The commands we will now discuss are executed from the Program Mode, but they too function to load and save information to your tape. They simply do it in a different format. To begin, we will review the different commands for working with data files, and then we will work with some programs employing these commands.

OPEN, INPUT#, PRINT# and CLOSE

In order to prepare your cassette for reading or writing information from within a program, the tape file must first be "prepared" with an OPEN statement. The format is as follows:

    OPEN N,1,(Ø,1 or 2),"FILE NAME"

1) First, "N" can be any integer from 1 to 255 to reference the file. For example, you might want to reference your file with number 21 (but any number between 1 and 255 would do just as well); so you would write:

        OPEN 21,etc.

2) Second, since the device is the cassette recorder, the second number would be "1". Your cassette is always addressed as "1" and your disk as "8".

        OPEN 21,1,etc.

3) Third, your file is prepared for reading with a 0, and writing with a 1 or a 2. If you want to write with an End-Of-File marker, use a "1", and for an End-Of-Tape marker use a "2".

        OPEN 21,1,0,etc. <-Read a file.
        OPEN 21,1,1,etc. <-Write a file with an End-Of-File marker.
        OPEN 21,1,2,etc. <-Write a file with an End-Of-Tape marker.

4) Fourth, provide a reference name for your file. For example, let's say you want to save your sprite data of a rocket you made, called "SPRITE ROCKET". You would write

        OPEN21,1,1,"SPRITE ROCKET"

or

        OPEN21,1,2,"SPRITE ROCKET"

To read that data, you would write,

        OPEN21,1,0,"SPRITE ROCKET"

It may appear to be somewhat involved, but once you get used to it, it is very simple. At the same time, it is quite flexible as well, since it is possible to open a number of different files simply by giving them different names. But usually you will want to CLOSE a file before OPENing another. To close a file, just enter CLOSE and the file number. In our example, we would enter:

        CLOSE21

So while there is a lot to remember in OPENing a file, there is not much when it comes to CLOSEing one.

The next command involves writing data to tape. Using the PRINT# command we can do this. The format for PRINT# is

        PRINT#,N,D

where "N" is the file number and "D" is the data. For instance, sticking with our example, to print a number or string to tape, we would enter:

        PRINT#21,etc.

If our data were strings, we would enter:

        PRINT#21,A$

or if numeric

        PRINT#21,A (or A% for integers)

It is important to remember that PRINT# is not the same as PRINT, and you cannot substitute a question mark (?) as is possible when using PRINT. That is, if you entered ?#, you'd get an error when you ran the program even though when you LISTed it, it would appear as PRINT#. Just to show you, enter the following:

        10 ?#1,5
        20 PRINT#1,5

RUN the program and you will get ?SYNTAX ERROR IN 10. Now, RUN 20, and you will get ?FILE NOT OPEN ERROR IN 20. The format in line 20 is correct, but since the file is not open you get an error. Now LIST the program, and lines 10 and 20 look identical! This is one case where LIST will not help in debugging a program. You must remember to write out PRINT# whenever you use it instead of using the "?" shortcut.

In the same way that PRINT# "prints" data to your tape, INPUT# "inputs" information into your computer *from* the tape. It has the same format as PRINT# using the OPENed file's number and reads in numeric or string variables.

        INPUT#21,A (or A% for integer numbers) <- Numbers
        INPUT#21,A$ <-Strings

Finally, we have the GET# statement which is formatted exactly like INPUT#, but like the GET command, it gets only 1 character at a time.

However, it can read commas, colons and other characters which INPUT#
cannot. It will not be used very much since most applications will want
more than a single character, but when you want to read special characters not available with INPUT#, GET# will come in handy.

At this point we have commands to open a file, read from or write to a file
and close a file. However, before we continue, there is a special variable,
ST, which we have to examine. The variable ST is reserved for checking
your tape to see if it is finished entering data. If ST = 0, then more data
is coming in. The End-Of-File or End-of-Tape marker has not yet been
read. Therefore, we can loop back to read more data using ST within an
IF/THEN statement. For example, the following format can be used

```
20 INPUT#21,A$
30 PRINT A$
40 IF ST = 0 THEN 20
```

Line 40 checks to see if there is more data, and if there is , it loops back
to line 20 to get it.

Now that we have seen all of the commands for reading and writing files
from and to tape, let's take a look at an application. We might as well use
a practical application; so we will make a list of our friends' phone numbers. Whenever we want to call a friend, just read the list from tape. First,
we must create a list to enter names and save them to tape. After we have
done that, we will write a program to retrieve the names and numbers.

```
10 PRINT CHR$ (147)
20 REM *** ENTER DATA ***
30 INPUT "HOW MANY NAMES TO ENTER"; N%
40 PRINT : DIM  NA$(N%), PH$(N%)
50 FOR I = 1 TO N%
60 PRINT "NAME#"; I ; : INPUT" (FIRST LAST)"; NA$(I)
70 INPUT "PHONE(XXX-XXXX)"; PH$(I)
80 NEXT I
100 REM *** SAVE DATA TO TAPE ***
110 OPEN1,1,1,"FRIENDS' PHONES"
120 FOR I = 1 TO N%
130 PRINT#1,NA$(I)
140 PRINT#1,PH$(I)
150 NEXT I
160 CLOSE1
```

To use this program, get a blank tape and rewind your cassette. RUN the program, and you will be prompted to PRESS RECORD & PLAY ON TAPE when you have entered all the names and numbers you want. As soon as you press the play and record buttons, your screen will go blank and your tape recorder spindles will begin turning. When all the information is saved, the recorder will stop and the screen will reappear indicating that all your data has been saved. (Tape storage is relatively slow compared to disks, so to save time it is suggested to use just a few names (3 or 4) at first.)

Now, let's see if everything worked out according to plan. To do that we need a program to read our data, and we will use INPUT# to read the names and numbers. Since both the names and phone numbers were saved as strings, we can do the whole thing with a single string variable we will call DA$ for "DATA STRING." (Remember to rewind your tape before RUNing this program!)

```
10 PRINT CHR$(147)
20 OPEN1,1,0,"FRIENDS' PHONES"
30 INPUT#1,DA$
40 PRINT DA$
50 IF ST = 0 THEN GOTO 30
60 CLOSE1
```

When you RUN this program, you will be prompted to PRESS PLAY ON TAPE. When you do so, the screen will go blank, and after a bit your text screen will reappear with all the names and phone numbers you entered. At this point you may say, "Now just a minute here! I entered that data as two different string arrays, and this program read only a single string variable! What happened to the arrays and how was it possible to get all that information back with a single variable?"

The answer to that question can be seen in how the data is stored and what our program did. While the file was OPENed, we INPUT# whatever data came along. As soon as it was in memory, we PRINTed it with our BASIC PRINT statement, *not* the PRINT# statement we use to print information to tape. The computer did not care whether the data entered into memory was a name or phone number, only a string, and as soon as that string was in memory it PRINTed to the screen. However, since the screen was blank, we could not see it being printed. In line 50 the program checked to see if there was more information in the file and if there was, it simply picked up and printed the next string, regardless of whether it was a name or a phone number. To test this, simply enter PRINT DA$ from the immediate mode, and the last entry will be printed to the screen.

Now, let's make our program a little fancier and more useful. If you use this program to store friends' phone numbers, the list will eventually cover more than a single screen. Therefore, you will be able to see only the last screenful of names and phone numbers. What we need is a program to search for and find a specific name and then close the file and print the name and number to the screen as soon as it has been located.

```
10 PRINT CHR$(147)
20 INPUT "NAME TO LOCATE";NA$
30 OPEN1,1,0, "FRIENDS' PHONES"
40 INPUT#1,DA$
50 IF DA$ = NA$ THEN GOTO 100
60 IF ST = 0 THEN GOTO 40
70 PRINT "NAME NOT FOUND"
80 CLOSE1
90 END
100 REM ** PRINT OUT NAME AND NUMBER ***
110 PRINT DA$ : REM PRINT THE NAME FOUND
120 INPUT#1,DA$: REM GET THE NUMBER
130 PRINT DA$ : REM PRINT THE NUMBER
140 CLOSE1
```

Now you have a handy program for storing names and numbers to tape and retrieving a single name and number you want to call. The next problem is updating your file without having to re-enter all of the names. That is, once you have made your phone list, you may want to add new names but you do not want to key in all the names you already have on your list. Can this be done? Yes, but first we have to read all the names into memory from tape and then write them back to tape. There are several ways this can be done, and our example is simply one way. We will do the following:

1. Load all the names and numbers on the tape into an array.
2. Input the new names and numbers on the end of the array.
3. Rewind the tape and resave the old and new data to tape.

```
10 PRINT CHR$(147)
20 DIM NA$(30), PH$(30) : REM DIM VALUE SHOULD BE
NUMBER OF NAMES ON LIST PLUS THE NUMBER OF NAMES
YOU WISH TO ADD
30 OPEN1,1,0,"FRIENDS' PHONES"
40 N = 0 : REM INITIALIZE COUNTER VARIABLE
50 INPUT#1,NA$(N)
60 INPUT#1,PH$(N)
```

```
70 N = N+1
80 IF ST = 0 THEN 50
90 CLOSE1
100 REM *** NEW DATA ENTRY ***
110 INPUT "HOW MANY NEW NAMES";NN
120 FOR I = (N+1) TO (N+NN)
130 INPUT "NAME";NA$(I)
140 INPUT "PHONE";PH$(I)
150 NEXT I
200 REM *** COMBINE OLD AND NEW DATA AND PUT IT ON
TAPE ***
210 NP = N + NN : REM COMBINED TOTAL OF ALL NAMES
220 OPEN 1,1,1,"FRIENDS' PHONES"
230 FOR I = 0 TO NP
240 PRINT#1,NA$(I)
250 PRINT#1,PH$(I)
260 NEXT I
270 CLOSE1
```

Make sure to rewind your tape as soon as all of the old data are loaded. In fact, it would probably be a good idea to insert a line to remind you. So add,

```
105 PRINT CHR$(147) : PRINT "REWIND TAPE NOW!" : PRINT
: INPUT "PRESS RETURN TO CONTINUE";RT$
```

That ought to remind you.

Now let's go back to see how we can save sprite information on tape. Also, we will see how we can load the information from tape and execute a program using the tape data. There is a word of caution in order, however. Sometimes there is more information on the tape than we want, and so it is important to load into memory just what we want and ignore everything else. This is a little inconvenient since we have to keep an eye on all of our data and know how many pieces of data make up our sprite. However, since that information is necessary anyway, our job is not too difficult.

To get started, we will create a sprite and save it to tape. We'll make one which looks something like a rocket.

```
10 PRINT CHR$(147) : REM *** CREATE SPRITE ***
20 DIM RS(63)
30 FOR I = 0 TO 32 : READ RS(I) : NEXT
```

```
40 DATA 30, 0, 0, 31, 0, 0, 31, 128, 0, 31, 255, 192, 31, 255,
240, 31, 255, 248
50 DATA 31, 255, 240, 31, 255, 192, 31, 128, 0, 31, 0, 0, 31, 0,
0
60 FOR I = 33 TO 62 : RS(I)=0 : NEXT I : REM FILL IN THE
REST OF THE SPRITE BLOCK WITH BLANKS (0'S)
100 *** REM BEGIN DATA STORAGE TO TAPE ***
110 OPEN1,1,1, "ROCKET SPRITE"
120 FOR I = 0 TO 62
130 PRINT#1,RS(I)
140 NEXT I
150 CLOSE1
```

We created the sprite just as we would if it were part of a program to run
the sprite. However, to insure that no "garbage" got into our sprite block,
we filled the remaining empty "boxes" in our block with "0's." When we
load the data from tape, we will know that no matter what sprite is to be
loaded, there are 63 (0 to 62) pieces of information to be loaded. This
takes the guess work out of loading sprites from tape. By using the maximum number of bytes in a sprite block, the smallest or largest sprite will
still be 63 bytes. This is because we filled in the empty bytes with 0's to
bring the total to 63 if the sprite was less than 63.

Now, let's load the sprite from tape and run it in a program. Be sure to
save the following program, for with it you can load from tape any sprite
you want and run it. This will save a good deal of time since, rather than
having to write a sprite routine every time you want to run a different sprite,
just load the program, set your cassette tape at the beginning of a sprite
and run the program. You can do this with any sprite you want.

```
10 PRINT CHR$(147)
20 BG = 53248 : TU = BG + 21 : S1 = 2 : L = 2040 : SS =
832 : SL = 13
30 X1 = BG + 2 : Y1 = BG + 3
40 REM *** END VARIABLE DEFINITION BLOCK ***
50 REM
100 REM *** READ DATA FROM TAPE ***
110 OPEN1,1,0,"ROCKET SPRITE" : REM YOU CAN LOAD ANY
SPRITE YOU WANT
120 DIM R(64)
130 FOR I = 0 TO 62
140 INPUT#1, R(I)
150 NEXT I
160 CLOSE1 : REM ALL DATA READ INTO MEMORY SO CLOSE
```

```
THE TAPE FILE
200 REM *** SPRITE CREATION BLOCK ***
210 FOR J = 0 TO 62
220 POKE SS + J, R(J)
230 NEXT J
240 POKE TU,S1
250 POKE L + 1, SL
260 POKE Y1, 100
270 FOR H = 0 TO 255
280 POKE X1, H : NEXT H
290 GOTO 270
```

No doubt you recognize our sprite program from Chapter 7, but instead of reading DATA statements to get the sprite values, it does it from tape. Note we did not use the ST variable to check to see if the data was completely read in, but instead we closed the file as soon as we had loaded 63 sprite values. This is to eliminate the possibility of any extra "noise" that might creep in from the tape. Also, it should be pointed out that it is possible to load multiple sprites using this method. This is possible by either reading multiple sprites saved to a single file, or, more usefully, sprites from different files. Simply remember to use all of the methods for manipulating and creating sprites we discussed in Chapter 7 with the only difference being that we get our data from tape rather than from DATA statements.

Sequential Files and the Disk System

If you do not have a disk system, you can skip this section and go on to the next chapter. However, if you are considering purchasing a disk drive for your COMMODORE-64, the following material will be of interest. In many respects storing data on disks is similar to storing it on tape except the storage and retrieval process is much quicker. In fact, all of our examples in the previous section can be operated with the disk system with only a few minor changes in the format. Therefore, to get started, we will see how we can store data to disks using a slightly different format than we did with tape. To do this we will examine the OPEN, CLOSE, INPUT#, PRINT# and GET# commands for disk.

OPEN — To open a disk channel, we access the device number "8" instead of "1" as we did with the tape. Having initialized the disk with the file number "15", we will OPEN another file number, say "9". Thus, we would enter

```
OPEN9,8,etc.
```

Instead of using code numbers 0, 1 and 2 to write, read or write End-of-Tape, we use READ and WRITE, or more simply, R and W. However, we format it differently. We OPEN the file beginning with the file number and the device number and then enter the secondary address, and the rest of our file handling commands are in quotation marks. The secondary address should not be 15, which is used in error handling, or 0 and 1 which are used by the operating system for loading and saving programs. The secondary address can be any number from 2 to 14. We will use "9" to keep things simple.

OPEN9,8,9,etc.

We begin the quotation marks with the drive number, "0" in the case of a single drive, followed by a colon and then the file name.

OPEN9,8,9,"0: FRIENDS' PHONES,etc."

Next, we enter the type of file we will be using. For the time being we will use sequential files, indicated by SEQ. Finally we enter READ or WRITE, depending on whether we want to save information to disk (WRITE) or retrieve it from disk (READ). Thus, our file OPENing routine would look like this:

OPEN9,8,9, "0: FRIENDS' PHONES, SEQ, WRITE"

Fortunately, INPUT#, PRINT# and GET# numbers use the same format as we did with tape. The number following each command is the secondary address. So, if we wanted to PRINT# in our example, we would write,

PRINT#9

since "9" is the secondary address. (Note: The number "9" is also the primary address, and by using the same number for both the primary and secondary addresses, we can minimize confusion.)

Now to see how all of this goes together, we will re-do our original "FRIENDS' PHONES" program we created for tape. The data entry block is identical, and so we will only do the block which saves the information to disk.

```
100 REM *** SAVE DATA TO DISK ***
110 OPEN9,8,9, "0:FRIENDS' PHONES, SEQ,WRITE"
120 FOR I = 1 TO N%
130 PRINT#9, NA(I)
140 PRINT#9, PH(I)
150 NEXT I
160 CLOSE9
```

As can be seen, the main difference between tape and disk is in the format in Line 110. Otherwise, the disk and tape writing format is identical. Likewise in retrieving information from disk, there are more similarities than differences between tape and disk. Also note that we were able to use the ST variable with disk I/O (input/output) as we were with tape.

```
10 PRINT CHR$(147)
20 OPEN9,8,9, "0:FRIENDS' PHONES, SEQ,READ"
30 INPUT#9,DA$
40 PRINT DA$
50 IF ST = 0 THEN GOTO 30
60 CLOSE9
```

To save some time, you can substitute "S" for "SEQ" and "R" for "READ". With these abbreviations Line 20 would read:

```
20 OPEN9,8,9, "0:FRIENDS' PHONES, S,R"
```

Similarly, it is possible to do the same with the other file status words, but you can never use abbreviations with file names.

Before going on to some more techniques using the disk system, there is a different technique for updating files than used with tape. As you remember from our tape program, we first read in all the data from our old file, added new data, then rewound the tape, and simply wrote over the old material. The same technique works with a disk, but instead of rewinding, we use a special format when OPENing the file when we prepare to write over it. The following block shows how this is done. Note again the similarities and differences between it and the one we used for tape.

```
200 REM *** COMBINE OLD AND NEW DATA AND PUT IT ON
DISK ***
210 NP = N + NN : REM COMBINE TOTAL OF ALL NAMES
220 OPEN9,8,9,"@ 0:FRIENDS' PHONES, S, W"
230 FOR I = 0 TO NP
240 PRINT#9, NA$(I)
250 PRINT#9, PH$(I)
260 NEXT I
270 CLOSE9
```

The key to overwriting an existing file is the "@" symbol. You will remember that in SAVEing over any existing file on disk we used the same format.

Now that we have seen how to do a number of programs individually, let's make a single program which will 1) Write files, 2) Read a single file or all the files, and 3) Add to a file. However, instead of using names and phone numbers, let's use names and addresses.

```
10 PRINT CHR$(147) : RESTORE : CLR
20 PRINT "***"; CHR$(18);"FILE MASTER"; CHR$(146); "***"
30 PRINT : FOR I = 1 TO 5: PRINT I"–" : PRINT :NEXT
40 PRINT CHR$(19): PRINT : PRINT : FOR I = 1 TO 5 : READ
D$ : PRINT SPC(5); D$ : PRINT : NEXT
50 DATA CREATE NEW FILE, ADD TO EXISTING FILE, READ
ALL FILES, READ SINGLE FILE
60 DATA EXIT
70 PRINT : PRINT CHR$(18); "CHOOSE BY NUMBER";
CHR$(146)
80 GET A : IF A < 1 THEN 80
90 ON A GOTO 100, 200, 400, 500, 700
100 REM *** CREATE A FILE ***
110 PRINT CHR$(147) : PRINT : PRINT
120 INPUT "HOW MANY NAMES"; N%
130 OPEN9,8,9, "0:ADDRESS LIST,S,W"
140 PRINT#9,N% : REM ENTER NUMBER OF NAMES IN FILE
150 DIM NA$(N%), AD$(N%), CT$(N%), SA$(N%), ZI$(N%)
160 FOR I = 1 TO N%: GOSUB 1000 : GOSUB 2000 : NEXT
170 CLOSE9
180 GOTO 10
200 REM *** ADD TO EXISTING FILE ***
210 PRINT CHR$(147) : PRINT : PRINT
220 INPUT "NUMBER OF NAMES TO ADD"; NN%
230 OPEN9,8,9, "0:ADDRESS LIST,S,R"
240 INPUT#9,N%: REM SEE HOW MANY NAMES ARE IN
EXISTING FILE
250 NP% = N% + NN%
260 DIM NA$(NP%), AD$(NP%), CT$(NP%), SA$(NP%),
ZI$(NP%)
270 FOR I = 1 TO N% : GOSUB 3000 : NEXT
280 CLOSE9
290 OPEN9,8,9, "@0:ADDRESS LIST,S,W"
300 PRINT#9, NP%
310 FOR I = (N% + 1) TO NP% : GOSUB 1000 : NEXT
320 FOR I = 1 TO NP% : GOSUB 2000 : NEXT
330 CLOSE9
340 GOTO 10
400 REM *** READ SUBROUTINE ***
410 OPEN9,8,9, "ADDRESS LIST,S,R"
420 INPUT#9,N%
430 DIM NA$(N%), AD$(N%), CT$(N%), SA$(N%), ZI$(N%)
440 FOR I = 1 TO N% : GOSUB 3000 : NEXT
450 CLOSE9
```

```
460 FOR I = 1 TO N% : GOSUB 4000 : NEXT
470 PRINT : PRINT "HIT ANY KEY TO CONTINUE"
480 GET A$ : IF A$="" THEN 480
490 GOTO 10
500 REM *** SEARCH SUBROUTINE ***
510 PRINT CHR$(147)
520 INPUT "NAME TO FIND"; NA$
530 OPEN9,8,9, "ADDRESS LIST,S,R"
540 INPUT#9,N%
550 DIM NA$(N%), AD$(N%), CT$(N%), SA$(N%), ZI$(N%)
560 FOR I = 1 TO N%: GOSUB 3000
570 IF NA$(I) = NA$ THEN GOSUB 4000
580 NEXT
590 CLOSE9
600 PRINT: PRINT: PRINT: PRINT "HIT ANY KEY TO CONTINUE"
610 GET AN$ : IF AN$ = "" THEN 610
620 GOTO 10
700 REM *** EXIT ***
710 END
1000 REM *** INPUT SUBROUTINE ***
1010 PRINT "NAME#";I;
1020 INPUT NA$(I)
1030 INPUT "ADDRESS"; AD$(I)
1040 INPUT "CITY"; CT$(I)
1050 INPUT "STATE"; SA$(I)
1060 INPUT "ZIP CODE"; ZI$(I)
1070 RETURN
2000 REM *** PRINT# SUBROUTINE ***
2010 PRINT#9,NA$(I)
2020 PRINT#9,AD$(I)
2030 PRINT#9,CT$(I)
2040 PRINT#9,SA$(I)
2050 PRINT#9,ZI$(I)
2060 RETURN
3000 REM *** INPUT# SUBROUTINE ***
3010 INPUT#9,NA$(I)
3020 INPUT#9,AD$(I)
3030 INPUT#9,CT$(I)
3040 INPUT#9,SA$(I)
3050 INPUT#9,ZI$(I)
3060 RETURN
4000 REM *** PRINT SUBROUTINE ***
4010 PRINT NA$(I) : PRINT AD$(I): PRINT CT$(I);", ";SA$(I);
" "; ZI$(I)
4020 RETURN
```

Now that was a long program! When writing such a program, it is a good idea to save your file about every 10-15 lines so if you accidentally lose it, you can retrieve most of your work. It is important to note several aspects of this program, including a new command, CLR. The CLR command clears all variables and arrays. That is important in this kind of program since you may want to do different things with it while it is in memory. For example, you may want to add to your address list and then locate a single name. By clearing the variables and arrays every time you go back to the menu, you will not have incorrect values.

Another important aspect to note is how the program is blocked into subroutines. Not only does this make it easier to read, but you can save a good deal of programming time by such organization. For example, in both the "READ" and "SEARCH" subroutines, the "INPUT#" subroutine is used. Thus, instead of having to key in the INPUT# commands more than once, the program simply jumps to the single subroutine. In the next chapter we will add a subroutine to print out the names and addresses to a printer, and instead of re-writing the entire program, all it takes is adding on another subroutine!

A final item you may have wondered about is using a string array for Zip Codes, ZI$(n). Why didn't we use a real variable? Well, a characteristic of BASIC language is the propensity to drop leading "0's" with real and integer variables and arrays. If your Zip Code is 07734, you wouldn't want your computer to say it was "7734". By using a string array, we retain the leading "0".

Summary

In this chapter we learned how to save a lot of time by saving files to tape and disk. Data can be saved to your cassette tape for use later within a program. This is handy since it allows you to enter data at one time and then use it later without having to key in the data all over again. Of course this can be done within a single program using READ and DATA statements, but the user is stuck with that program for using the data. By storing it on tape, it is possible to use it in many different programs. This is especially handy with sprites you have created.

Using a disk system, it is possible to store data in sequential files much like saving data to tape. However, disks access the data much faster than tapes, and it is possible to have a single program do several different things with data files on disks. The "File Master" program showed how a single program could be used to create, append, and read single or multiple files. Care has to be taken to keep everything straight with such a program, but using sequential files increases the power of your computer a great deal. The practical applications of such programs are immense.

CHAPTER 9

You and Your Printer

Introduction

By now you should be used to "outputting" information to your screen, cassette or disk. When you write in PRINT "HELLO" you "output" to your screen. When you SAVE or PRINT# something, you "output" to your tape or disk. In the same way that you access your screen, tape or disk, you can access your printer. It is simply another "output" target. However, you cannot LOAD, INPUT or in some other way get anything from your printer as you can from your keyboard, tape or disk. (How are you going to get the ink off the paper and back into memory?)

The procedures for getting material out to your printer and using your printer's special capabilities require certain procedures not yet discussed, however. Therefore, while much of what we will examine in this chapter will not be new in terms of the language of commands, it will be new in terms of how to arrange those commands. Also, we will see how we can use the printer in ways which have been done poorly using the screen. For example, no matter how long a program listing is, it can be printed out to the printer, while long listings on the screen scrolled right off the top of the screen into Never-Never land. Likewise, in Chapter 8, we made a handy little program for storing friends' phone numbers and another one for storing names and addresses. With a printer we can print-out our phone numbers or run off mailing labels with commands which output information to the printer.

There are a lot of printers on the market for computers. However, to keep things simple and to show the maximum use of your COMMODORE-64 with a printer, all examples will be with Commodore's VIC-1515 printer. This printer will provide all graphic and text features you will need, and it is easily interfaced to the COMMODORE-64 system. Besides, it is a very inexpensive printer. If you have another printer and an interface for the COMMODORE-64, then you will have to rely heavily on your printer's manual. Unfortunately, many printer manuals are not very good for beginners since they tend to use highly technical descriptions of how to interface and operate their printers. Therefore, pay special attention to the codes used to turn on or off special features of your printer. This is usually done with a CHR$ command from BASIC, and so, usually all you will have to do is to follow the instructions in this book using the appropriate code from your printer's manual.

BEFORE YOU BUY A PRINTER!!

The most important aspect in purchasing a printer is making certain it will interface with your COMMODORE-64. Many times over-enthusiastic salespersons will tell buyers all the qualities of a printer and naively believe they can be used on any computer. This is simply not true! In order for a printer to work with a computer, it must have the proper interface, and the best printer in the world will not work with your COMMODORE-64 without such an interface. Therefore, when you buy a printer other than one made specifically for your COMMODORE-64, make sure to buy the proper interface for it. The only *certain* way to insure the printer works with a COMMODORE-64 is to have it demonstrated with your computer. The VIC-1515 and VIC-1525 printers by COMMODORE will work with the COMMODORE-64, but otherwise you should have the printer's ability to work with your computer shown to you.

Printing Text On Your Printer

The first thing you will want to do with your printer is to print some text in "hardcopy." ("Hardcopy" is a really impressive term computer people use to talk about print-outs on paper. Use the term and your friends will be amazed.) Like your cassette tape and disk drive, it is necessary to first go through a number of steps to channel information to your printer. Let's review those steps first.

OPEN — First, you OPEN a channel to your printer. On the VIC-1515, there is a switch in the back to make the device number 4 or 5. We will use the "4" in our examples, so check to make sure the switch is flipped to "4" before proceeding. (Remember on your disk drive the device number is "8.") The sequence for OPENing the channel to your printer is to enter a number between 1 and 255 (we'll use lucky "7") and the device number,4. Here's how:

        OPEN7,4

Now your printer is ready to receive instructions to "7", the logical file number we used.

CMD — The CMD command tells your computer to send output to your printer. You must use the file number (7 in this case) and not the device number (4). For example, enter

        CMD7

and you will hear your printer "crank" up and print-out READY, as it usually prints to the screen. However, you will notice that it did *not* print READY to your screen. Now enter

        FOR I = 1 TO 10 : PRINT : NEXT

and your printer will feed your paper 10 lines, just as it would to the screen had you not directed output to the printer with the CMD command. Until you turn off the output to your printer it will go there instead of to your screen.

There is an important output difference between your printer and your screen which should be noted. Enter

        FOR I = 1 TO 80 : PRINT "X";: NEXT

and 80 "X's" will be printed to your printer in a single line. If the same command were printed to your screen, it would take up two lines. This is because your printer outputs 80 columns while your screen outputs only 40.

PRINT# — You will remember that we use PRINT# in programs where we want to print our information to our tape or disk. Well, with your printer the same principle applies also. Let's say that you want to print-out only a few things in a program and do not want everything going to the printer. If you used CMD everything would go to the printer which would normally go to the screen. However, using PRINT# only the information following the PRINT# would. For example, suppose you want to have your screen prompt you with "Name?" and as soon as you enter the name it is printed to your printer, you would want to use PRINT#. The format is

        PRINT#7, NA$

or

        PRINT#7, "CHARLIE TUNA"

or

        PRINT#7, 12345

Let's try a little program to print names to the printer to show how PRINT# can be used in programs where you want to use both the screen and printer.

        10 PRINT CHR$(147)
        20 PRINT : PRINT : PRINT "TURN ON YOUR PRINTER"
        30 PRINT : PRINT : PRINT "HIT ANY KEY TO CONTINUE"
        40 GET A$: IF A$ = "" THEN 40
        50 PRINT CHR$(147)

```
60 OPEN7,4
70 INPUT "NAME TO PRINT";NA$
80 PRINT#7,NA$
90 INPUT "ANOTHER(Y/N)";AN$
100 IF AN$ = "Y" THEN 70
110 CLOSE7
120 END
```

CLOSE — The final command in accessing your printer is CLOSE. As we can see in the above program, it closes the channel to the printer and turns it off. For the most part CLOSE works pretty much the same way as it does with the tape and disk systems; however, there is an important protocol involved. Before you CLOSE the channel to the printer, you must enter PRINT#{fn} first. Therefore, if you OPEN a channel to the printer and use the CMD command, you must *first* PRINT# before issuing a CLOSE command. For example,

```
OPEN7,4
CMD 7
PRINT "HELLO HELLO"
PRINT#7
CLOSE7
```

If you issued the CLOSE command without the PRINT# command, you would run into problems.

Listing Programs

Since listing programs to one's printer is a good way to de-bug a program or send it to a friend, it would be convenient to have a utility program with which we do just that. So, let's write a program which will list your program to the printer. We will keep it short so that we can tack it onto the beginning of a program. To get started, load a program into memory and then add the following lines:

```
1 OPEN7,4
2 CMD7
3 LIST 5-
4 END
```

When you RUN this program, it "turns on" the printer and LISTs a program from line 5 to the end of the program. When you are finished, enter PRINT#7 and CLOSE7 to close the channel and the file. Unfortunately, you cannot turn off the CMD command from within the program using PRINT# and

CLOSE as we did using only the PRINT# command. So be sure to turn it off from the immediate mode after a listing.

CHR$ To the Rescue

The secret to using printers is in understanding what their control codes mean and how to use those codes. For example, the following is a partial list of codes provided with a CENTRONICS 737 printer:

MNEMONIC	DECIMAL	OCTAL	HEX	FUNCTION
ESC,SO	27,14	033,016	1B,0E	Elongated Print
ESC,DC4	27,20	033,034	1B,13	Select 16.7 cpi
ESC,DC1	27,17	033,021	1B,11	Proportional Print

Now, for most first-time computer owners, that could have been written by a visitor from another planet for all the good it does. However, there is important information in those codes and, once you get to know how to use them, it is relatively easy.

To get started, forget everything except the "Decimal" and "Function" columns. Now, taking the first row, we have decimal codes 27 and 14 to get elongated print. To tell your printer you want elongated print you would use CHR$(27) + CHR$(14). To kick that into your printer you would do the following:

        1. OPEN7,4
        2. PRINT#7, CHR$(27) + CHR$(14) + "MESSAGE"

If you have a Centronics 737 or 739 printer, that would have printed the string "MESSAGE" in an elongated print. Likewise, for the condensed printing 16.7 cpi (characters per inch), you would have entered CHR$(27) + CHR$(20) and for the proportional type face, CHR$(27) + CHR$(17). Once you get the decimal code, just enter that code to the printer and it will do anything from changing the type-face to performing a backspace function.

With other printers the same is true, but let's get back to the VIC-1515 printer we have been examining since it was designed with Commodore computers in mind. As we will see, like the Centronics printers or any other, the VIC-1515 and VIC-1525 also use CHR$ commands to access the printer's different abilities. Let's look at the various CHR$ commands associated with the VIC-1515:

CHR$	FUNCTION
10 & 13	Line feed
8	Graphic Mode
14	Double width
15	Back to standard
16	Address of start print position
27	Escape (used in conjunction with other codes)
145	Cursor up
17	Cursor down
18	Reverse printing
146	Turn off reverse

To see how the CHR$ functions work, we will use a simple program which will print-out your name. Since we already know how to print-out normal text, we will begin with expanded text. Looking at our chart, we see that CHR$(14) will expand our print-out; so we will use it in our program. (Notice the *lack* of punctuation marks after the comma following the PRINT#7.)

```
10 PRINT CHR$(147)
20 OPEN7,4 : REM OPEN CHANNEL 7 TO DEVICE 4 (YOUR
PRINTER)
30 INPUT "YOUR NAME"; NA$
40 PRINT#7, CHR$(14) NA$ : REM NOTE POSITION OF
CHR$(14) AFTER PRINT#7
50 PRINT#7, CHR$(15) : REM RETURN TO NORMAL PRINT
60 CLOSE7
```

RUN the program and print-out some names and note the expanded characters. (Try that on your typewriter!)

Now we have not done very much with upper and lower case so far, but in printing text to your printer, there are many times you will want to have upper and lower case characters. For example, in printing out names, you may want your printer to print-out,

Captain John W. Smith

instead of

CAPTAIN JOHN W. SMITH

but we need a special CHR$ command to do that. With the VIC-1515 printer the CURSOR DOWN mode, CHR$(17), will allow us to print upper and lower case. To do this, change lines 40 and 50 in our above program to the following:

    40 PRINT#7, CHR$(17) NA$: REM PRINTS IN CURSOR DOWN
    MODE
    50 PRINT#7, CHR$(145) : REM RETURNS TO CURSOR UP
    MODE

Now, press the COMMODORE key and SHIFT key simultaneously to put your computer into the upper/lower case mode and RUN the program. If you used the shift key for upper case and the non-shifted keys for lower case, your printer gave you both upper and lower case. If you tried that before we made the program changes, even if you had your computer in the upper/lower case mode, your print-out would have given you graphic characters for the shifted ones instead of upper case. Go ahead and try it with the original program to see for yourself.

Another trick is to use both upper and lower case and the expanded mode together. You just have to change the program so that both CHR$ commands are there together. Again, change lines 40 and 50 to the following:

    40 PRINT#7, CHR$(17) CHR$(14) NA$
    50 PRINT#7, CHR$(145) CHR$(15) : REM RETURN TO CUR-
    SOR UP AND STANDARD PRINT

When you RUN this program, you will see that it is possible to have more than a single non-standard (i.e. non-default) mode operating simultaneously. On some printers, such as the EPSON MX-80FT with GRAFTRAX

PLUS, it is possible to not only have expanded print but also italicized, condensed, double strike, emphasized and super/subscript type faces and any combination of them together. Using CHR$, all of the different type styles can be used separately or in combination with one another. Finding the "CURSOR UP/DOWN" mode on other printers, however, may be tricky since they were not made specifically for the COMMODORE-64. (Remember to get a demonstration at the store where you buy your printer!)

Now that we have seen different ways to operate the type faces on the printer, let's do something practical. We will make a mailing label program for the VIC-1515/1525 printer. Various label manufacturers make adhesive labels with tractor-feed margins so that you can put them into your printer just like your paper. Our program will make labels that will print the addressee's name in expanded upper/lower case, the address in regular upper/lower case, and the city, state and zip code in upper case only.

```
10 PRINT CHR$(147) : PRINT CHR$(14) : REM SHIFT TO
UPPER/LOWER CASE
20 OPEN7,4
30 INPUT "NAME"; NA$
40 INPUT "ADDRESS"; AD$
45 PRINT CHR$(142) : REM SHIFT TO UPPER CASE
50 INPUT "CITY"; CT$
60 INPUT "STATE"; SA$
70 INPUT "ZIP CODE" ; ZI$
100 PRINT#7, CHR$(17) CHR$(14) NA$
110 PRINT#7, CHR$(15) CHR$(17) AD$
120 PRINT#7, CHR$(145) CT$ ", " SA$ " " ZI$
130 CLOSE7
```

As you will see when you RUN this program, the screen shifts to the mode your print-out will be in. This helps the user see on the screen what he/she will get on the printer. Note that *different* CHR$ codes are used to shift the upper/lower case mode on the screen and on the printer. For example, CHR$(142) shifts the screen to upper/lower case while CHR$(17) shifts the printer to that mode.

In order for the program to be more practical, we will need a few line feeds at the end of the printing so that your labels can be properly aligned. Depending on the size of your mailing labels, you will need a greater or fewer number of line feeds. Insert the following line into your program and adjust the size of the loop to align your labels properly.

125 FOR I = 1 TO 3 : PRINT#7 : NEXT : REM CHANGE "3"
TO THE CORRECT NUMBER OF LINE FEEDS FOR YOUR
LABELS

In Chapter 8, we promised to insert a subroutine in the "FILE MASTER"
program to print out the names and addresses to your printer. Well, that's
just what we're going to do. To make the changes, load your "FILE MAS-
TER" program into memory and make the following additions or changes
in the program. (Good grief! Don't rewrite the whole thing!)

```
470 PRINT "HIT ANY KEY TO RETURN TO MENU OR 'P' FOR
PRINTER"
485 IF A$ = "P" THEN GOSUB 5000
525 INPUT "SCREEN(S) OR PRINTER(P)";OP$
570 IF NA$(I) = NA$ AND OP$ = "S" THEN GOSUB 4000
575 IF NA$(I) = NA$ AND OP$ = "P" THEN GOSUB 6000
5000 REM *** PRINTER SUBROUTINE ***
5010 OPEN7,4
5020 CMD7
5030 FOR I = 1 TO N% : PRINT NA$(I) : PRINT AD$(I)
5040 PRINT CT$(I); ", ";SA$(I);" "; ZI$(I) : PRINT
5050 NEXT
5060 PRINT#7
5070 CLOSE7
5080 RETURN
6000 REM *** PRINTER SUBROUTINE FOR ***
6010 REM *** SINGLE FILE ***
6020 OPEN7,4
6030 CMD7
6040 PRINT NA$(I) : PRINT AD$(I) : PRINT CT$(I);", "; SA$(I);
" "; ZI$(I)
6050 PRINT#7
6060 CLOSE7
6070 RETURN
```

Sometimes you do not want your print-out to begin at the left hand side
of your paper or label. To position the starting point of your text, you use
CHR$(16) and the number of spaces from the left you wish to begin
printing. There are a number of different ways of doing this, but the simplest is to first print CHR$(16) and the starting position in quotes along
with what you want printed. You must use a two-digit number; thus, if you
want to begin 5 spaces from the left, you must indicate it with "05" instead
of "5." For example, try the following:

```
OPEN7,4
PRINT#7, CHR$(16)"05DOES THIS COMPUTE?"
CLOSE7
```

As you will see when you execute the above commands, your printer will only print out "DOES THIS COMPUTE?" and not the "05" even though it was in quotation marks. That was because the first two-digit number encountered after the CHR$(16) was the "05." Now add another "5" so that the line reads,

```
PRINT#7, CHR$(16)"055DOES THIS COMPUTE?"
```

and you will get "5DOES THIS COMPUTE?" Thus, after the second digit everything is treated as information to be printed out.

In some cases you may want to indicate the number of spaces using CHR$ instead of numbers within quotes. For example, you may wish to print text at different positions determined by a loop and want your next position in relation to the last, and so the position is determined by CHR$(I), with "I" being the current loop position. This can be done, but it is tricky because the CHR$ must be the ASCII value for the number. For example, a "05" looks like this:

```
CHR$(0) CHR$(53)
```

Using the above example, you would print,

```
PRINT#7, CHR$(16) CHR$(0) CHR$(53) "DOES THIS
COMPUTE?"
```

Therefore, if computing the position using a loop, it is necessary to determine the position in terms of both the first and second digit as an offset of the loop value. For most applications, it is best simply to enter the number of positions within the quotation marks of the message to be printed.

Before going on to printer graphics, we will examine how to use positioning in a program. This is useful in making lists where columns are important. For example, we can make a list of items for a garage sale. The first column will be the item for sale, the second column the asking price for the item, and the third column the actual price for which the item sold. We will use INPUT statements so that all items can be entered from the keyboard and used with an actual garage sale. (Who knows when you will want to use it? So why not make it useful!)

```
10 PRINT CHR$(147)
20 PRINT : PRINT : INPUT "HOW MANY ITEMS"; N% : DIM
IT$(N%), AP(N%), SP(N%)
30 PRINT : FOR I = 1 TO N%
40 PRINT "ITEM #"; : INPUT IT$(I)
50 INPUT "ASKING PRICE"; AP(I)
60 INPUT "SELLING PRICE"; SP(I)
70 PRINT
80 NEXT
100 REM *** PRINTER FORMAT ROUTINE ***
110 OPEN7,4
120 PRINT#7, "ITEM"; CHR$(16) "15ASKING PRICE";
130 PRINT#7, CHR$(16) "35SELLING PRICE"
140 PRINT#7, CHR$(10) : REM LINE FEED
150 FOR P = 1 TO N%
160 PRINT#7, IT$(P)
170 PRINT#7, CHR$(16) CHR$(49) CHR$(53) "$"; AP(P)
180 PRINT#7, CHR$(16) CHR$(51) CHR$(53) "$"; SP(P)
190 NEXT
200 CLOSE7
```

There are a couple of things to note in this program. First of all, notice how we employed CHR$ code to indicate the positioning of the printed text in lines 170 and 180. The combination of those codes is the same as the "15" and "35" enclosed in quotations in lines 120 and 130. Second, we used the CHR$(10) for a line feed. We could have used PRINT#7 without any code following it to get the same results, but there will be times when you may wish to insert a line feed into the middle of a line and CHR$(10) will come in handy. To make a really neat program, see if you can figure out how to have the program compute the totals of the asking price and selling price of the items. Also, it might be an interesting addition to have a fourth column which keeps a tally of the differences between the asking and selling prices. This is something which you should be able to work out on your own! (Hint: Create a fourth array.)

Printing Graphics

Now that we have seen how to print text, we will look at graphics printing. The simplest graphics to print are those from the keyboard. Using the CURSOR UP mode, CHR$(145), we can print out the graphics from the keys. For example, from the Immediate mode try the following,

```
OPEN7,4
PRINT#7, CHR$(145) "{COMMODORE-KEY-B}"
CLOSE7
```

That will print out a "checkerboard" character just like the one on the left side of the key. Now, since the default mode is CURSOR UP, it is unnecessary to enter CHR$(145) every time you print a graphic character but, just to be sure, you should have it somewhere in your program.

To see all the different graphic characters from your keyboard, run the following program:

```
10 PRINT CHR$(147)
20 OPEN7,4
30 FOR I = 96 TO 127 : REM CHR$ RANGE OF SET #1
40 PRINT#7, CHR$(145) CHR$(I)
50 NEXT I
60 FOR J = 161 TO 191 : REM CHR$ RANGE FOR SET #2
70 PRINT#7, CHR$(145) CHR$(J)
80 NEXT J
90 CLOSE7
```

All of the characters on your keyboard were printed out for you, but with patience you could have done the same from the keyboard. The CHR$(145) is a bit superfluous, and you can get the same results if you remove it. However, if CHR$(17) is there, you will have mostly blanks since that is the "upper/lower" case, or CURSOR DOWN mode.

Making Your Own Graphic Characters On the Printer

In Chapter 7 we showed how to create sprites using a binary coding translation. Now we will do the same thing with printer graphics, but it is far simpler. First of all, we will only be using a 7 by 7 matrix instead of a 24 by 21 matrix so there are far fewer calculations. The VIC-1515 printer can actually make graphic characters in a 7 by 480 (!) matrix, but we will stick with the 7 by 7 matrix to keep it simple. To get started, instead of sending you off for some graph paper, we will make our own graph for our matrix on the printer, explaining the process as we go along.

To begin, we use CHR$(8) to initiate the graphics mode. Then we "build" a concatenated CHR$ that contains our graphic image. Since the bits are added on the basis of the vertical position of each "pin" in the printer head, we will be adding vertical "dots" instead of horizontal ones as we did with sprite graphics. However, we will be using the same concepts as with sprite graphics. The following is an outline of our 7 by 7 matrix:

```
 1  __  __  __  __  __  __  __
 2  __  __  __  __  __  __  __
 4  __  __  __  __  __  __  __
 8  __  __  __  __  __  __  __
16  __  __  __  __  __  __  __
32  __  __  __  __  __  __  __
64  __  __  __  __  __  __  __
+128
```

By inserting "dots" into the blanks, we can create a figure, and this is translated to a way in which the COMMODORE-64 can understand by a vertical total of the positions the dots are in and adding 128. For example, if we draw a square, we would have the first and last columns filled and the top and bottom rows filled. Beginning with the first column, the value would be 1 + 2 + 4 + 8 + 16 + 32 + 64 + 128, equaling 255. The next 5 columns would have a dot at the top and bottom. A dot in the top row would be 1 and one in the bottom row would be 64, and adding the 128 we would get 193. The last column would be the same as the first, 255. Therefore, we would want to create a CHR$ that has the following values:

        255 193 193 193 193 193 255

for our box figure. To do this we could have a line that reads as follows:

        BOX$ = CHR$(255) + CHR$(193) + CHR$(193) + CHR$(193)
        + CHR$(193) + CHR$(193) + CHR$(255)

but that (whew!) would take a lot of time. Instead it would be a lot simpler to READ in the values as DATA statements as we did with the sprites and concatenate the string, such as,

```
FOR I = 1 TO 7
READ GRAPHICS
GR$ = GR$ + CHR$(GRAPHICS)
NEXT
DATA 255,193,193,193,193,193,255
```

Now let's put it all together into a program.

```
10 PRINT CHR$(147)
20 FOR I = 1 TO 7 : READ GRAPHICS
30 GR$ = GR$ + CHR$(GRAPHICS)
40 NEXT
```

```
50 OPEN7,4
60 PRINT#7, CHR$(8) GR$
70 CLOSE7
100 DATA 255,193,193,193,193,193,255
```

When you RUN this program, a little box will be printed. Nothing very exciting, I admit, but now let's see how we can use that little box to make a matrix to create new characters. The following program will make a 7 by 7 matrix for you and only requires making a few changes in the above program:

```
10 PRINT CHR$(147)
20 FOR I = 1 TO 7 : READ GRAPHICS
30 GR$ = GR$ + CHR$(GRAPHICS)
40 NEXT
50 OPEN7,4
52 FOR Y = 1 TO 7
54 FOR X = 1 TO 7
60 PRINT#7, CHR$(8) GR$;
62 NEXT X
64 PRINT#7
66 NEXT Y
70 CLOSE7
100 DATA 255,193,193,193,193,193,255
```

If you printed out the 7 by 7 matrix, you can see that, while it is functional, it really printed more than was necessary. We only need single-sided dividers between the cells. Besides, even though having the single box is handy for making all different kinds of shapes, we might as well create the exact graphics we need. However, if we let the computer do the "figuring" for us, it can be relatively simple. To begin we will break up the task into simple parts. First of all, we know that a straight vertical line is CHR$(255). We will call it E$ since it "encloses" the sides of our box. We also know that CHR$(193) will give us a top and bottom to our box, but if we use it to make a matrix, we will have double lines separating our rows. Therefore, we will only need a top line to begin with. That's easy since the top dot is "1" so we just have to add "128" for CHR$(129). We need five of those dots to create our top line, so we will create that with a FOR/NEXT loop of 5. (Remember in our 7 x 7 boxes, the E$ figure will take a top position dot at either end.) Finally, at the end of our matrix we are going to need a bottom line. Here, instead of drawing a single bottom line, we will draw a bottom line of boxes made up of E$ and CHR$(193), the latter to be designated as TB$ (for "top/bottom"). Therefore, the plan is to first draw 6 lines of boxes with a top only and then, for our seventh line, we will draw a row with both tops and bottoms. It is important to notice that we are now using graphic figures much larger than our 7 x 7 matrix! Here's our improved program:

```
10 PRINT CHR$(147)
20 E$ = CHR$(255)
30 FOR I = 1 TO 5 : T$ = T$ + CHR$(129) : NEXT
40 FOR I = 1 TO 5 : TB$ = TB$ + CHR$(193) : NEXT
50 OPEN7,4
60 FOR Y = 1 TO 6
70 FOR X = 1 TO 7
80 PRINT#7, CHR$(8)E$ T$
90 NEXT X
100 PRINT#7, E$ : REM PUTS AN END ENCLOSURE ON
BOXES
110 NEXT Y
120 FOR X = 1 TO 7
130 PRINT#7, CHR$(8)E$ TB$;
140 NEXT
150 PRINT#7, E$
160 CLOSE7
```

Now that you have a better idea of what can be created, print up a batch of matrixes and design some original printer graphics! You always wanted your own logo, and now you can do it!

Repeat That Graphic!

The final element we will examine with your printer is the graphic repeat one. Using CHR$(26) it is possible to make any number of graphic characters repeat. However, the format for using repeat requires some care. Use the following steps:

1. Get into the graphics mode with CHR$(8)

2. Issue the repeat command with CHR$(26)

3. Enter the number of repeats within a CHR$ command. Note: This is different from what we saw with the position command. You do not put in the ASCII code for the number of repeats, but instead the actual number of times you want a graphic repeated. For example, if you want a graphic to repeat 20 times, you would use CHR$(20).

4. Enter the graphic character, usually followed by the CHR$ code for a semi-colon <CHR$(59)> so that the repetition will occur on the same line.

Now let's make a simple program which will give us a "bar" of varying lengths. This will show how you might begin a program which will make a bar graph with bars of different lengths to represent your data.

```
10 PRINT CHR$(147) : PRINT : PRINT
20 INPUT "LENGTH OF BAR"; N
30 RP$ = CHR$(8) + CHR$(26) + CHR$(N) : REM GRAPH
ICS + REPEAT + NUMBER OF REPEATS
40 VL$ = CHR$(255) + CHR$(59) : REM OUR VERTICAL
LINE PLUS A SEMI-COLON
50 OPEN7,4
60 PRINT#7, RP$ VL$
70 CLOSE7
```

Notice how fast the bar is produced on your printer using the repeat function. Experiment with the command and mix it together with other printer commands to produce anything you want to see in black and white.

Summary

When you got your printer, you may have thought the only thing you could print was text in the same way a typewriter does. However, as we saw, that was just the beginning. Besides printing text, it is possible to generate different style type faces, position the text wherever you want and even print graphics. Not only can you print the graphics from the keyboard, you can also create your own printer graphics. Typewriters just cannot do that!

The secret to using printers with your COMMODORE-64 is the CHR$ function. In some ways CHR$'s are used as ASCII code in exactly the same way as they are when output is to the screen; but in other ways they are used either as special printer functions or, within certain sequences, to produce print-outs. Unfortunately, it is not possible to simply access your printer and have it automatically put what's on the screen onto paper. However, by planning your program around output to the printer, just about anything printed to the screen can be printed to your printer.

CHAPTER 10

Program Hints and Help

Introduction

Well, here we are at the last chapter. We've covered most of the commands used for programming in BASIC on the COMMODORE-64 and many tricks of the trade. If you are seriously interested in learning more about your computer and using it to its fullest capacity, there's still more to learn. In fact, this last chapter is intended to give you some direction beyond the scope of this book.

First, we will introduce you to the best thing since silicone — COMMODORE-64 Users Groups. These are groups that have interests in maximizing their computer's use. Second, I would like to suggest some periodicals that can help you learn more about your COMMODORE-64 computer. Third, we will examine some languages besides BASIC that can be used on your COMMODORE-64. BASIC has many advantages, but like all computer languages, it has its limitations and you should know what else is available.

Next, we will examine some more programs. There will be listings of programs that you may find useful, fun, or both. The ones included were chosen to show you some applications of what we have learned in the previous nine chapters, enhancing what you already know. We will also look at different types of programs you can purchase. These are programs written by professional programmers to do everything from making your own programming simpler, to keeping track of your taxes. Later, we will examine some hardware peripherals to enhance your COMMODORE-64.

Commodore-64 User Groups

Of all of the things you can do when you get your COMMODORE-64, the most helpful, economical and useful is joining a COMMODORE-64 User Group. Not only will you meet a great group of people with COMMODORE-64 computers, but you will learn how to program and generally what to do and what not to do with your computer. The club in your area will probably be one with other COMMODORE computer owners, such as PET and VIC-20 users.

Usually the best way to contact your COMMODORE-64 User Group is through local computer stores. Often stores selling COMMODORE-64 computers will have application forms and some even serve as club meeting sites. Other microcomputer clubs in your area may also have COMMODORE-64 users in them, but if there is not an COMMODORE club, join a general computer group. The help you will get will be worth it.

To start your own COMMODORE-64 User's group, post a notice, meeting time and site in your local computer store. Write to one of the following:

> Commodore User Clubs
> c/o Editor
> *Commodore Magazine*
> 487 Devon Park Drive
> Wayne, PA 19087
>
> *COMPUTE!'s Gazette*
> P.O. Box 5406
> Greensboro, NC 27403
> Attn: Commodore Users' Groups
>
> *COMMANDER*
> P.O. Box 98827
> Tacoma, WA 98498
> Attn: Users' Group Listing

and ask them to publish a notice that you want to start a COMMODORE-64 club in your area. Your club will then be listed in the magazine(s) you notify and other people in your area will soon join up. If you live in an area with just a few COMMODORE-64 owners, or in a relatively small town, it would be a good idea to affiliate with one of the larger groups. Probably the best bet would be to join the following group:

> TORONTO PET USERS GROUP
> Department "D"
> 1912 A Avenue Road, Suite 1
> Toronto, Ontario, Canada M5M 4A1

The Toronto group has over 3000 free programs for the various computers made by Commodore along with a club newsletter to keep you informed. The dues are $20, but you will get back a lot more than that in programs and information.

Another way to get in touch with fellow COMMODORE-64 users is via a VICMODEM. Dial up the computer bulletin boards in your area and look for messages pertaining to COMMODORE-64's; usually you can get in contact with other users very quickly this way. (Ask for the PMS {Public Message system} numbers at your local computer store.) If you don't see any references to the COMMODORE-64, leave a message for people to get in touch with you.

Commodore-64 Magazines

There are several periodicals with information about the COMMODORE-64. Some microcomputer magazines are general and others are for the COMMODORE-64 only. When you're first starting, it is a good idea to stick with the ones dedicated to the COMMODORE-64 since there are different versions of BASIC for non-COMMODORE-64 computers. When you become more experienced you can choose your own, but to get started there are several good ones with articles exclusively on the COMMODORE-64. These are as follows:

Commodore: The Microcomputer Magazine
Commodore Business Machines, INC.
The Meadows
487 Devon Park Drive
Wayne, PA 19087

Commodore is a monthly publication with a wide variety of articles and programs for the COMMODORE-64. Here you will find programming techniques, tips for beginners, new hardware and software available and various applications. Articles range from the simple to the technical, so regardless of your level of expertise, you will find this extremely useful. Subscriptions are $15.00 per year for 6 issues.

Powerplay
Commodore Business Machines, INC.
The Meadows
487 Devon Park Drive
Wayne, PA 19087

A second magazine for your COMMODORE-64 is *Powerplay*, a quarterly publication dedicated to the more recreational uses of your computer. The articles and programs in this magazine are primarily for home uses of your computer, ranging from games to telecommunications. It is very educational and helpful for novices. Subscriptions are $10.00 per year.

Compute!'s Gazette
P.O. Box 5406
Greensboro, NC 27403

Compute!'s Gazette is dedicated to the COMMODORE-64 and VIC-20. *Compute!'s Gazette* will provide you with programs and programming techniques that can be applied to your computer. Additionally, it has several general articles on programming, hardware and software that you will find useful. Finally, there are numerous bargains on software and peripherals to be found in the magazine. Subscriptions are $15 for 12 issues.

Commander
The Monthly Journal for Commodore Computer Users
P.O. Box 98827
Tacoma, WA 98498

Commander magazine has an excellent selection of programs, reviews, tutorials and articles for Commodore computers, including the COMMODORE-64, VIC-20 and PET. The wide range and high quality of the material in this magazine will be an immense help to beginners in programming. Subscriptions are $22 for 12 issues.

Other Useful Publications

In addition to the above four magazines, there are several others that you may find useful. Publications such as *Compute!, Creative Computing, Byte, Interface Age, Popular Computing* and *Personal Computing* all have had articles about the COMMODORE-64. The best thing to do is go through the table of contents in the various computer magazines in your local computer store. This will tell you at a glance if there are any articles or programs for the COMMODORE-64. As more and more clubs begin springing up, club newsletters can often be an invaluable source of good tips and programs for your computer. They are a resource that should not be overlooked.

Commodore-64 Speaks Many Languages

Beside BASIC, your computer can be programmed and can run programs in several other languages. In some cases, special hardware devices are required to run the languages and special software is required as well. We'll look at some of these other languages.

Assembly Language

Assembly language is a "low level" language, close to the heart of your computer. It is quite a bit faster than BASIC and virtually every other language we will discuss. To write in Assembly language, it is necessary to have an "assembler" to enter code. This language gives you far more control over your COMMODORE-64 than BASIC, but it is more difficult to learn and an Assembly program takes more instructions to operate than BASIC. (However, the object code is more compact, taking up fewer sectors on your disk.) The ASSEMBLER 64 assembler by Commodore, Inc. requires the 1541 disk drive since the macro assembler and supporting programs are on disk. It includes two machine language monitors, editors and loaders. One of the best assemblers now on the market for the COMMODORE-64 is

MERLIN
Southwestern Data Systems
P.O. 582
Santee, CA 92071

In addition to having a full set of macros, editor and other standard assembler features, *Merlin* comes with an excellent monitor for examining machine code in your programs and ROMs. The manual will help you get started programming in Assembly language. All programs written with *Merlin* can be automatically saved to disk as binary files.

Also, you might want to look at

MAE (Macro Assembler Editor)
Microtech
P.O. Box 102
Langhorne, PA 19047

To learn how to program in Assembly language, the following books were found to be the most useful:

1. COMMODORE 64 PROGRAMMER's REFERENCE GUIDE. (Commodore) This book can be purchased from your local book or computer store or from:

Commodore Business Machines, INC.
The Meadows, 487 Devon Park Drive
Wayne, PA 19087

This is a most useful book for programming with the COMMODORE-64 assembler.

2. *COMPUTE!'S* MACHINE LANGUAGE FOR BEGINNERS by Richard Manfield (Greensboro, N.C.: *COMPUTE!* Books) $12.95. This book includes an assembler written in BASIC and explains how to make the jump from BASIC to Machine/Assembly language. It is written in a very friendly manner and includes many Assembly language programs. It is a general 6502 microprocessor Assembly language book, but is shows how to use the opcode with the COMMODORE-64's 6510 CPU as well.

3. INSIDE THE COMMODORE 64 (French Silk, P.O. Box 207, Cannon Falls, MN 55009). This book was written to go with French Silk Assembler/Editor/Loader/Decoder/Monitor that comes with the book. It was prepared exclusively for the COMMODORE-64 and it is a good way to get started with both instructions and an assembler. The book and assembler come in one package for $54.95. (Disks are $5 extra.)

To help debug your programs, Pterodactyl Software, 200 Bolinas Road #27, P.O. Box 538, Fairfax, CA 94930, makes a Debugger for COMMODORE-64. It will step through a Machine/Assembly program and help you find the bugs.

A final utility you may want to examine while learning Machine/Assembly language is AUTOHEX/PEEKPOKE. This program lets the user copy a machine program into a BASIC program. Once in BASIC, it can easily be listed to examine the hexadecimal code. Also, if the program is written in hex, the user can load and run it with AUTOHEX/PEEKPOKE. Available on cassette tape for only $5.00 from David M. Conley, 10571 Kerrigan Ct., Santee, CA 92071.

HIGH AND LOW LEVEL LANGUAGES

When computer people talk of "high" and "low" level languages, think of high level being close to talking in normal English and low level in terms of machine language, e.g. binary and hexadecimal. Assembly language is a low level language, one notch above machine level. The other languages we will discuss are high-level.

PASCAL

Pascal is a high-level language originally developed for teaching students structured programming. It is faster than BASIC, but is not as difficult to master as Assembly language. It is probably the most popular high level language next to BASIC. You will find different versions of Pascal, but the language is fairly well standarized so that whatever version of Pascal you purchase will work with just about any Pascal program. The following is available for the COMMODORE-64:

> KMMM PASCAL
> Microtech
> P.O. Box 102
> Langhorne, PA 19047

There are several books available so one can learn how to program in Pascal, the following having been found to be among the best:

> 1. ELEMENTARY PASCAL: LEARNING TO PROGRAM YOUR COMPUTER IN PASCAL WITH SHERLOCK HOLMES. By Henry Ledgard and Andrew Singer. (New York: Vintage Books.) This is a fun way to learn Pascal since the authors use Sherlock Holmes type mysteries for you to solve with Pascal. It is based on

the draft standard version for Pascal called X3J9/81-003 and may be slightly different from the version you have, but only slightly so.

2. PASCAL FROM BASIC. By Peter Brown. (Reading, MA: Addison-Wesley, 1982). If you understand BASIC, this book will help you make the transition from BASIC to PASCAL. It is written with the PASCAL novice in mind but assumes the reader understands BASIC.

FORTH

FORTH is a very fast high-level language, developed to create programs that are almost as fast as Assembly language, but take less time to program. Faster than Pascal, BASIC, Fortran, COBOL, and virtually every other high-level language, FORTH is programmed by defining "words" that execute routines. New words incorporate previously defined words into FORTH programs. The best part of FORTH is that several versions are public domain. The FIG (FORTH Interest Group) FORTH version is in the public domain and if you are handy with Assembly programming, you might even be able to install your own. The following packages are available for the COMMODORE-64.

1. fullFORTH+ $100.00
   Microtech
   P.O. Box 102
   Langhorne, PA 19047

2. C64-FORTH $99.95
   Performance Micro Products
   770 Dedham Street. S-2
   Canton, MA 02021

The best source to learn about what's available is through the publication, *FORTH Dimensions* (see below) and your magazines where COMMODORE-64 products are advertised.

Good books on learning FORTH are now plentiful. For learning FORTH, the following are recommended:

1. FORTH PROGRAMMING by Leo J. Scanlon (Indianapolis: Howard S. Sams & Co., 1982). This book uses the FORTH-79 and FIG-FORTH models as standards, thereby providing the user with the most widely distributed versions of FORTH. This is a well organized and clear presentation of FORTH.

2. STARTING FORTH by Leo Brodie (Englewood Cliffs: Prentice-Hall). Well written and illustrated work on FORTH for beginners. Uses a combination of words from FIG, 79-Standard and polyFORTH.

3. POCKET GUIDE TO FORTH by Linda Baker and Mitch Derick. (Reading, Mass.: Addison-Wesley, 1983). This is a handy alphabetical reference to the FORTH vocabulary and a good explanation of FORTH's structure. It is a good for beginners since each FORTH instruction is explained clearly and is easy to find. However, it should only be considered as a supplement to one of the above books.

4. *FORTH Dimensions*. Journal of FORTH INTEREST GROUP, P.O. Box 1105, San Carlos, CA 94070. This periodical has numerous articles on FORTH and tutorial columns for persons seriously interested in learning the language.

CP/M

For the COMMODORE-64, there are several excellent CP/M programs available. In fact, CP/M has one of the largest available public domain libraries of any language. In order to get CP/M for your computer, it is necessary to have a cartridge with a Z-80 microprocessor; there are several available. Many business programs, including word processors and data base programs, are available in CP/M, and for those primarily interested in business and professional applications, CP/M is certainly something you will want to look into. The COMMODORE-64 has a plug-in Z-80 pack that simply pops into the back of your computer. It comes with a disk with a CP/M operating system. When running CP/M on your COMMODORE-64, the Z-80 microprocessor takes over operations from the 6510. With the Commodore Z-80 cartridge, you essentially have 2 computers! The Commodore Z-80 and Z-80 Reference Guide are available at your Commodore dealer. With CP/M, you can then install virtually any program running on CP/M, including other languages such as Pascal and FORTH.

Miscellaneous Languages

Besides the above languages, it is possible to get disks with COBOL, FORTRAN, LOGO, PILOT and other languages for specialized and general applications. LOGO and PILOT, for example, are used in teaching children programming, while COBOL is used primarily in business applications. Before you spend time, money and effort on another language, it is highly recommended that you carefully examine your needs. If your main interest is in developing your own programs, first learn BASIC thoroughly and explore what you can do with it. If it fits your needs, and its relatively slow speed is sufficient for your uses, then your time will be better spent improving your programming skills in BASIC. If your main interest is in using application programs, then the language capability depends on the programs you are using. Most importantly, in this context, is whether or not you use CP/M. If you do, then you will need some kind of Z-80 cartridge. Just about all other professionally produced programs will run on a COMMODORE-64 without any other added hardware. (This includes programs written in Pascal, FORTH, etc.)

Finally, if you find that programming in BASIC is most suitable for you, but you would like to speed up your programs, a simple way to do that is with a compiler. Essentially, a compiler is a program that transforms your code into a binary file that will run 4 to 5 times faster than COMMODORE-64 BASIC. All you do is write the program in BASIC, compile it, and then save the compiled program. From then on, you run your compiled program as a machine language program. The following compiler is now available for your COMMODORE-64.

> BASM COMPILER
> Computer Alliance
> 2115 Devonshire, Suite 132A
> Chatsworth, CA 91311

Sort Routines

These programs will sort strings for you. They represent different algorithms and you can see that certain algorithms work faster than others. The "Bubble Sort" is the simplest and slowest of the three for wholly unsorted lists, but it works very well with partially sorted lists. The "Shell Sort" and "Quick Sort 2" work much faster in general than the "Bubble Sort", but they use far more complex formulas. Test them to see which works best for your sorting needs. You will probably want to use these sorts in your programs that require some alphabetic manipulation.

Bubble Sort

```
10  PRINT CHR$(147)
20  INPUT "HOW MANY WORDS TO ENTER ";N%
30  DIM A$ (N%+1)
40  FOR N =1 TO N%
50  INPUT "ENTER WORD ";A$(N)
```

```
60  Z=Z+1
70  NEXT N
80  PRINT CHR$(147) : FOR I=1 TO 10 : PRINT : NEXT :
M$="ALPHABETIZING"
90  L=20−LEN (M$)/2 : PRINT CHR$(18);SPC(L);M$ : PRINT
CHR$(146)
100  REM ***********
110  REM BUBBLE SORT
120  REM ***********
130  T=N−1
140  FLIP=0 : FOR S=1 TO T : IF A$(S)<= A$(S+1) THEN 160
150  SWITCH$ = A$(S) : A$(S)= A$(S+1): A$(S+1)=
SWITCH$ : FLIP=1 : T=S
160  NEXT S :IF FLIP=1 THEN 140
200  REM *** OUTPUT TO SCREEN ***
210  REM *** IN ALPHABETICAL ORDER ***
220  FOR N = 2 TO Z +1
230  F=F+1
240  IF F> 22 THEN GOSUB 300
250  PRINT A$ (N)
260  NEXT N
270  END
300  REM *** STOP WHEN SCREEN FILLS ***
310  PRINT CHR$(18);"HIT ANY KEY TO CONTINUE "
320  GET AN$: IF AN$ ="" THEN 320
330  F=0 : PRINT CHR$(146)
340  RETURN
```

Shell Sort

```
10  PRINT CHR$(147)
20  INPUT "HOW MANY WORDS TO ENTER ";N%
30  DIM A$ (N%+1)
40  FOR N =1 TO N%
50  INPUT "ENTER WORD ";A$(N)
60  V=V+1
70  NEXT N
80  PRINT CHR$(147) : FOR I=1 TO 10 : PRINT : NEXT :
M$="ALPHABETIZING"
90  L=20−LEN (M$)/2 : PRINT CHR$(18);SPC(L);M$ : PRINT
CHR$(146)
100  REM **********
110  REM SHELL SORT
120  REM **********
```

```
130  Y=1
140  Y=2*Y : IF Y <= N THEN 40
150  Y=INT(Y/2):IF Y=0 THEN 200
160  FOR X=1 TO N−Y : Z =X
170  K=Y+Z : IF A$(Z) <= A$(K) THEN 190
180  SWITCH$=A$(Z):A$(Z)=A$(K) :
A$(K)=SWITCH$:Z=Z−Y : IF Z>0 THEN 170
190  NEXT X : GOTO 150
200  REM *** OUTPUT TO SCREEN ***
210  REM *** IN ALPHABETICAL ORDER ***
220  FOR N = 2 TO V +1
230  F=F+1
240  IF F> 22 THEN GOSUB 300
250  PRINT A$ (N)
260  NEXT N
270  END
300  REM *** STOP WHEN SCREEN FILLS ***
310  PRINTCHR$(18);"HIT ANY KEY TO CONTINUE "
320  GET AN$: IF AN$ ="" THEN 320
330  F=0 : PRINT CHR$(146)
340  RETURN
```

Quick Sort

```
10   PRINT CHR$(147)
20   INPUT "HOW MANY WORDS TO ENTER "; N%
30   DIM A$ (N% + 1)
40   FOR N =1 TO N%
50   INPUT "ENTER WORD ";A$(N)
60   Z = Z + 1
70   NEXT N
100  REM *** QUICKSORT 2 ***
110  PRINT CHR$(147)
120  S1 = 1
130  L(1) = 1
140  R(1) = N
150  L1 = L(S1)
160  R1 = R(S1)
170  S1 = S1 − 1
180  L2 = L1
190  R2 = R1
200  X$ = A$ ( INT ((L1 + R1) / 2))
210  C = C + 1
220  IF A$(L2) > = X$ THEN 250
```

```
230  L2 = L2 + 1
240  GOTO 210
250  C = C1
260  IF X$ > = A$(R2) THEN 290
270  R2 = R2 − 1
280  GOTO 250
290  IF L2 > R2 THEN 360
300  S = S + 1
310  T$ = A$(L2)
320  A$(L2) = A$(R2)
330  A$(R2) = T$
340  L2 = L2 + 1
350  R2 = R2 − 1
360  IF L2 < = R2 THEN 210
370  IF L2 > = R1 THEN 410
380  S1 = S1 + 1
390  L(S1) = L2
400  R(S1) = R1
410  R1 = R2
420  IF L1 < R1 THEN 180
430  IF S1 > 0 THEN 150
440  REM *** SORT COMPLETE ***
500  REM *** OUTPUT TO SCREEN IN ***
510  REM *** ALPHABETICAL ORDER ***
520  FOR N = 2 TO Z + 1
530  F = F + 1
540  IF F > 22 THEN GOSUB 1000
550  PRINT A$(N)
560  NEXT N
570  END
1000  PRINT CHR$(18);"HIT ANY KEY TO CONTINUE "
1010  GET AN$: IF AN$ = "" THEN 1010
1020  F = 0: PRINT CHR$(146)
1030  RETURN
```

Key Tricks

Before you read this, promise not to get angry. OK? All right, now you can read on. Up to this point we have not used a number of short-cuts available on your keys. This is because it was important for you to first get used to the commands and how to use them correctly. Also, as we will see, the short-cuts do not clearly show you what is happening on your computer as fully as writing out the commands.

In Appendix D of your COMMODORE-64 USER'S GUIDE there is a chart that shows you how to enter the first one or two letters of a command and then SHIFT the second or third letter to get the entire command. This will save you some time in programming, but it is difficult to read the command until you get used to it. For example, put a program into memory and enter "L {SHIFT-I} and RETURN. The command is the same as entering LIST except you only have to make two key presses instead of four. Now, clear memory and enter the following:

```
10  ? C {SHIFT-H} (147) : A$= "ALLRIGHT"
20  ? S {SHIFT-P} 10); R {SHIFT-I} (A$,5)
```

Before you RUN the program, can you guess what will happen? If you cannot, don't feel bad since it is confusing, especially the way it appears on the screen. When you RUN the program, it will clear the screen and print the message "RIGHT" 10 spaces from the left side of the screen at the top. Now LIST your program and all the commands are clear. These key short-cuts are handy in some cases and confusing in others. The LIST command is usually from the Immediate Mode and it is handy to use it in the abbreviated fashion, but until you become better acquainted with programming, these short-cuts may be more confusing than helpful. Use the ones you feel comfortable with, and introduce the short-cuts gradually.

USING WAIT

One of the statements we did not discuss is WAIT. The explanation for using WAIT is fairly complex and we will not go into it here, but it can be very useful in your programs. It works something like GET except there is no cursor on your screen, making for clean user initiated program control. Besides WAIT-ing for a keypress, WAIT can also be used with your joysticks for game development. However, we will just use it here to show how to stop a program until a key is pressed. Key in the following program and try it out.

```
10  PRINT CHR$(147)
20  FOR I = 1 TO 10 : PRINT : NEXT I
30  PRINT "<HIT ANY KEY TO CONTINUE>"
40  WAIT 197,64 : WAIT 197,64,64
50  PRINT : PRINT "YOU HAVE CONTINUED!"
```

To learn more about WAIT see Louis F. Sander's excelent article "All About Commodore's WAIT Instruction" pp. 153-158 in *Compute!* January 1983.

Function Keys

To the right of your keyboard are four keys we have not mentioned yet. They are called the "Function Keys" and are accessed by CHR$ values from 133 to 140. To use them, a "keyboard scan" is set up and when one of the "8" keys (4 non-shifted plus 4 shifted) is pressed, the program branches to a subroutine. They have applications where the user is expected to interact with the program from the keyboard but the other keys are used for INPUT of characters and keyboard graphics. For example, let's say you wanted to have a program that would enter names until a certain key was pressed. Since you would not want the key to be one with which you entered characters for the name you are entering, you could use the Function Keys. The CHR$ values from 133 to 140 are linked to the keys 1 through 8 with the non-shifted keys being from CHR$(133) to CHR$(136) and the shifted keys from CHR$(137) through CHR$(140). For example, CHR$(133) is for Function Key 1 (f1), CHR$(137) for "f2", CHR$(134) for "f3" and up to CHR$(140) for "f8." The following program illustrates how to set up a program to use the Function Keys. Only keys 1, 5 and 8 are used, with the program ending if key f5 is pressed.

```
10  PRINT CHR$(147)
20  GET A$
30  PRINT CHR$(19)
40  IF A$ = CHR$(133) THEN GOSUB 1000
50  IF A$ = CHR$(140) THEN GOSUB 2000
60  IF A$ = CHR$(135) THEN END
70  PRINT "CHOOSE FUNCTION KEY 1 OR 8"
80  PRINT "TO END PRESS FUNCTION KEY 5"
90  GOTO 20
1000  PRINT CHR$(147) : PRINT "YOU CHOSE
FUNCTION KEY 1"
1010  PRINT "HIT ANY KEY TO CONTINUE"
1020  WAIT 197,64 : WAIT 197,64,64
1030  PRINT CHR$(147) : RETURN
2000  PRINT CHR$(147) : PRINT "YOU CHOSE
FUNCTION KEY 8"
2010  PRINT "HIT ANY KEY TO CONTINUE"
2020  WAIT 197,64 : WAIT 197,64,64
2030  PRINT CHR$(147) : RETURN
```

Utility Programs

What's A Utility

Utility programs are programs that help you program or access different parts of your computer. In this section we will review some of the more useful utility programs available at this time.

1. The VicTree $89.95
($99.95 with Centronics standard printer cable.)
Skyles Electric Works
231E South Whisman Road
Mountain View, CA 94041

The VicTree plugs into the back of your COMMODORE-64 and provides you with an incredible range of utilities. You can do everything from renumber your programs to text editing with the VicTree. It will make programming simple and give you access to a full range of inexpensive parallel printers combined with the commands in the VicTree and printer cable. Program editing and disk access are greatly enhanced.

2. Basic Tools $16.95
COMM DATA
Computer House, Inc.
320 Summit Avenue
Milford, Michigan 48042

This inexpensive utility package for the COMMODORE-64 will renumber, append, delete a range of line numbers and perform several other handy debugging functions. It is available on cassette or disk.

If you join a COMMODORE-64 User Group, you will learn about a lot more utility programs and other's experiences with them. Like all other programs that you are thinking of buying, ask other users about them and get a demonstration of their use first!

Word Processors

Your COMMODORE-64 can be turned into a first class word processor with a word processing program. Word processors transform your computer into a super typewriter. They can do everything from moving blocks of text to finding spelling mistakes. Editing and making changes is a snap, and once you get used to writing with a word processor, you'll never go back to a typewriter again. This book was written with a word processor and it took a fraction of the time a typewriter would have taken. (Believe me, I've written 10 other books with a typewriter!)

There are some limitations with word processors. First, the COM-MODORE-64 screen displays only 40 columns. Since the standard page size is 80 columns, this bothers some people since what appears on the written page is different from what appears on the screen. However, since I write material that will be printed out in everything from 40 to 132 columns, the 40 columns do not bother me. If you want 80 columns for your screen, you can purchase adaptors that will provide 80 columns on the screen. Using an 80 column adaptor, you can see exactly what you will get when you print out your material. The following adaptors are among those available for the COMMODORE-64:

1. 80 COLUMN VIDEO $179.95
    Microtech
    P.O. Box 102
    Langhorne, PA 19047

2. 80 COLUMN BOARD
    Protecto Enterprizes
    Box 550
    Barrington, IL 60010

To give you some help in making up your mind, the following are some features you might want to look for in a word processor:

1. Find/Replace.
    Will find any string in your text and/or find and replace any one string with another string. Good for correcting spelling errors and locating sections of text to be repaired.

2. Block Moves.
    Will move blocks of text from one place to another. (e.g. Move a paragraph from the middle to end of document.) Extremely valuable editing tool.

3. Link Files.
    Automatically links files on disks. Very important for longer documents and for linking standardized shorter documents.

4. Line/Screen Oriented Editing.
    Line oriented editing requires locating the beginning of the line of text and then editing from that point. Screen oriented editing allows beginning editing from anywhere on the screen. The latter form of editing is important for large documents and where a good deal of editing is normally required.

5. Automatic Page Numbering.
    Pages are automatically numbered without having to determine page breaks in writing text.

6. Imbedded Code.
    In word processors, this enables the user to send special instructions directly to the printer for changing tabs, enabling special characters on the printer and doing other things to the printed text without having to set the parameters beforehand and/or having the ability to override set parameters.

These are just a few of the things to look for in word processors. As a rule of thumb, the more a word processor can do, the more it costs. If you only want to write letters and short documents, there is little need to buy an expensive word processor. However, if you are writing longer, more complex and wide varieties of documents, the investment in a more sophisticated word processor is well worth the additional cost. If you have specialized needs (e.g. producing billing forms), you will want to look for those features in a word processor. Therefore, while a word processor may not do certain things, it may be just what you want for your special applications. As with other software, get a thorough demonstration of any word processor on COMMODORE-64, before laying out your hard earned cash. EASY SCRIPT and WORD/NAME MACHINE from Commodore are simple word processors. EASY SPELL 64 can be used with EASY SCRIPT to automatically check the spelling in EASY SCRIPT files. The following are some other word processors you might want to examine:

1. SCRIPT 64 $139.95
Computer Marketing Services, Inc.
300 W. Marlton Poke
Cherry Hill, NJ 08002 (609) 795-9480
This full function word processor has a built-in 20,000 word dictionary to check your spelling! It is designed to support the 1541 disk drive and 1525 printer.

2. WORD PROCESSOR PLUS $25.00
William Robbins
Box 3745
San Rafael, CA 94912
Good for short documents such as letters and memos.

3. WordPro 3 Plus/64 $89.95
Professional Software Inc.
51 Fremont Street
Needham, MA 02194 (617) 444-5224
This is a good general purpose word processor. Among included features are automatic page numbers, math functions and global search and replace.

4. TOTL.TEXT 2.6 + CS $40.00
TOTL Software, Inc.
1555 Third Ave
Walnut Creek, CA 94596 (415) 943-7877
A combination word processing, mailing lists and label package with fast printing and loads. Compatible with 80 column boards.

As a cautionary note, word processors take a bit of time to learn to use effectively. It is possible to start writing text immediately with most word processors, but in order to use all of their features, practice is required. One of the strange outcomes of this is that once a user learns all the techniques of a certain word processor, he or she will swear it is the best there is! Therefore, avoid arguments about the best word processor. It's like arguing politics and religion. Also, if you have a printer, check to make sure a particular word processor will send text to your printer. This is especially true if you have a parallel printer adaptor.

Data Base Programs

When you need a program for creating and storing information, a "data base" program is required. Essentially, professionally designed data base programs are either sequential or random access files. When you use one, all you have to do is to use the pre-defined fields provided or create fields. For example, a user may want to keep a data base of customers. In addition to having fields for name and address, the user may want fields for the specific type of product the customer buys, dates of last purchase, how much money is owed, date of last payment, etc.

Probably more than most other packages, data base programs should be examined carefully before purchasing. Some of the more expensive data bases can be used with virtually any kind of application, but for example, if you're only going to be using your data base to keep a list of names and addresses to print out mailing labels, a data base program designed to do that one thing will usually do it better and for a lot less money. Some word processors, such as Commodore's WORD/NAME MACHINE and TOTL's TOTL.TEXT 2.6 + CS can be used as mailing list data base systems in addition to word processors; so you may not even need a data base program if your word processor can handle your needs. On the other hand, if your needs are varied and involve sophisticated report generation and changing record fields, then do not expect a simple, specialized program to do the job. Commodore's THE MANAGER is such a general data base program. It has the added advantage of being compatible with their word processors so that data base files can be loaded into your word processor. The following are some special and general use data base programs:

1. THE DATA MANAGER
Timeworks, Inc.
405 Lake Cook Road, Bldg. A
Deerfield, IL 60015 (312) 291-9200
An inexpensive general purpose data base program. Fields can be formatted by user.

2. THE 64 MAILING LIST $27.95 (c) $29.95 (d)
Galactic Software
P.O. Box 10516
San Jose, CA 95157 (408) 247-4434
Used for creating and maintaining mailing lists. Sorts and prints lists/labels on all fields.

3. DISK DATA MANAGER $89.95
MICRO SPEC
P.O. Box 863085
Plano, TX 75086 (214) 867-1333
General purpose data base system allowing up to 1200 records on a single disk.

There are several other data base programs, including public domain ones available through your club.

Business Programs

Business programs have such a wide variety of functions that it is best to start with a specific business need and see if there is a program that will meet that need. On the other hand, there are general business program that are applicable to many different businesses. Specific business programs include ones that deal only with real estate, stock transactions and nutritional planning. More general programs include "Electronic Spreadsheets," "Financial Planning," and, as discussed above, data base programs.

Commodore has five EASY FINANCE packages that cover a wide range of business decision-making and analysis problems. Also EASY CALC 64 by Commodore is a general use "spreadsheet" program that can be used to keep track of figures requiring a row/column calculation format. It also will create graphs and tables based on the calculations. The following are other business packages you may be interested in examining:

Texas Technical Services, Inc.
3115 W. Loop, S, Suite 26
Houston, TX 77027 (713) 965-9977
1. General Ledger $129.95
2. Payroll System $129.95
3. Accounts Payable $129.95
4. Accounts Receivable $129.95
5. Client Accounting $229.95

Micro Spec
P.O. Box 86385
Plano, Texas 75086 (214) 867-1333
1. Payroll System $99.95
2. Inventory Package $99.95
3. General Ledger $99.95
4. Checkbook Manager $69.95

CALC RESULT
Computer Marketing Services, Inc.
300 W. Marlton Poke
Cherry Hill, N.J.
This is a powerful spreadsheet program including graphic display to screen or printer, "three dimensional" overlap and color coordinated cells.

Unfortunately, business people often spend far too much for systems that do not work. They believe that if software and hardware costs a lot of money then, it must be better than a less expensive simpler system. This thinking is based upon a "You Get What You Pay For" mentality, and it leads to systems that are not used at all. Here is where a good dealer or consultant comes in handy. First, since computers are getting more sophisticated and less expensive, often you do *not* "Get What You Pay For" when purchasing a big expensive one. Often all the business person ends up with is a dinosaur system that is outmoded, too big and too expensive for the needs. Some computer dealers specialize in helping the business person. They will help set up the needed system in your place of business, help train office personnel and provide ongoing support. These dealers will charge top dollar for your system and supporting software, as opposed to the discount dealers and mail order firms; however, if you have any problems, you will have someone who will come and help you out. Since the COMMODORE-64 is so inexpensive to begin with, the extra money spent on buying from a business supportive dealer is well worth the little extra cost. Alternatively, there are several consultants for setting up your system. If you use a consultant, get one who is an independent without any connection to a vested interest in selling computers. Contact one through your phone book and tell him your want to set up a COMMODORE-64 system in your office and let him know exactly what your needs are. If they are familiar with your system, they will know the available software and peripherals you need. If they try to sell you another computer, that probably means they are unfamiliar with your system and it is a good idea to try another consultant. However, if you are told by several consultants that your needs cannot be met by a COMMODORE-64, then you may indeed need a larger system.

I do not mean to sound cynical, but I have encountered too many unhappy business people who bought the wrong system for their needs. One businessman said he paid $14,000 for a computer system that never did work for his requirements and finally bought a microcomputer system for about a tenth of the price and everything worked out fine. This does not mean that a business may not require an expensive mainframe to handle certain business functions and the COMMODORE-64 certainly has its limitations. Before you buy *any* system, make sure it does what you want and have it shown to you working in the manner you expect it to. Often you will find that the less expensive new micros like the COMMODORE-64 will actually work better than costly big machines.

Graphics Packages

In our chapter on graphics we discussed some of the COMMODORE-64's capabilities with graphics. However, certain uses require either highly advanced programming skills or a good graphics package. For example, it is possible to draw on the screen in hi-resolution graphics, just as you would with a palette. The pictures produced can then be saved to disk or printed out to your printer. Also, the sprite editor, such as the one that comes on the diskette or cassette with the DISK/CASSETTE BONUS PACK, is a great help in creating sprites. These programs allow you to concentrate on the graphics themselves, rather than the programming techniques necessary to produce them. Some other graphic packages available include:

1. SPRITE EDITOR $15 (c) $20 (d)
Software Creators
1628 La Corta
Lemon Grove, CA 92045
Powerful sprite editor allows user to have as many as 65 (!) sprites in memory simultaneously, reversible sprites, machine language subroutines for maximizing speed and many extras. Good program for game development.

2. '64 PENCIL $24.95
Dungeness Software
323 Lotzgesell Road
Sequim, WA 98382
High resolution graphic sketch pad. Draw with joystick to create graphic pictures on screen. Pictures can be dumped to Commodore 1525 printer with "DUNGENESS DUMP" included in program.

3. LIGHT PEN $29.95
CARDCO
313 Mathewson
Wichita, Kansas 67214 (316) 267-6525
Draws pictures to the screen directly with a light pen.

Hardware

The COMMODORE-64 is "expandable." That means you can add various attachments to it to make it do more than it does normally. In the back of your machine there are three ports where hardware extensions can be attached and on the right side there are two additional sockets for game paddles and/or a joystick. Game paddles and joysticks are used for games as well as other programs. For games, they guide rockets, space ships and characters against the forces of evil. However, they are also used for drawing graphics and input in other programs as well.

Other hardware attachments are interfaces for various peripherals. One, called an IEEE Interface, can connect up to 15 (!) devices to your COMMODORE-64. Three companies that make IEEE interfaces for the COMMODORE-64 are:

1. The Computer Works
   2028 West Camel Back Road
   Phoenix, AZ 85015 (602) 249-0611

2. Richvale Telecommunications
   10610 Bayview Plaza
   Richmond Hill, Ontario L4C 3N8 (416) 884-4165
   (IEEE Interface with BASIC 4.0)

3. Micro Systems Development, Inc.
   11105 Shady Trail Suite 104
   Dallas, TX 75229 (214) 241-3743

Another important peripheral you may want to consider is a parallel inter-face board. With these you can connect your COMMODORE-64 to many different low priced parallel printers. The following are available for your computer:

1. CPI COMMODORE-64 PARALLEL INTERFACE
   Micro Systems Development, Inc.
   11105 Shady Trail Suite 104
   Dallas, TX 75229 (214) 241-3743

2. (a) PARALLEL INTERFACE $19.95
   (b) INTELLIGENT PARALLEL INTERFACE $119.95
   Micro-Ware Distributing, Inc.
   P.O. Box 113
   Prompton Plains, N.J. 07444 (201) 838-9027
   The inexpensive PARALLEL INTERFACE (a) will connect your COMMODORE-64 to any parallel printer for dumping text to your printer. The INTELLIGENT PARALLEL INTERFACE (b) provides a full emulation of Commodore printers for print-ing text and graphics.

Like software, before you purchase an interface or peripheral, make sure it works with your computer! Unfortunately, many hardware attachments come with such poor documentation, that without someone to show you how to work it, it is almost impossible to get them to operate properly. Again, this is where a users group proves invaluable. Ask other members about their experiences before buying a peripheral.

Modems and Communications

One of the most exciting things you can do with your computer is to communicate with another computer. Not only can you communicate with another COMMODORE-64, but you can access other micros and even tie into big mainframes. With the COMMODORE-64 you are in luck, for with the VICMODEM by Commodore and the *right* software, you can inexpensively make such connections. Commodore makes two modems for the COMMODORE-64, the VICMODEM 1600 and the AUTOMODEM 1650. To be honest, the software that comes with the VICMODEM isn't so hot, and a lot of people have complained that they cannot get their VIC-MODEM working. However, since the price is so low ($48.95 in one discount store I visited), it seems a shame to give up on it. But, do not despair, for with good communications software, the VICMODEM is a terrific little device! I highly recommend the following communication package:

> SMART 64 TERMINAL $39.95
> Microtechnic Solutions, Inc.
> P.O. Box 2940
> New Haven, CT 06515
> With Smart 64 Terminal, you can transform BASIC programs into sequential files and send programs to your friends via your modem. It is possible to both upload and download programs, save them on disk and then convert them back to BASIC files to be RUN. The program is simple yet powerful, and it can be used to dump text to any serial printer.

Another good modem package that includes both the hardware and software necessary for communications is:

> HES MODEM $89.95
> Human Engineered Software
> 71 Park Lane
> Brisbane, CA 94005
> This package contains everything you need for modem communications with both high quality hardware and software.

Besides calling your friends and local bulletin boards FREE, you can also tap into some really big information systems for a price. Three such systems include THE SOURCE, COMPU-SERVE and DOW JONES NEWS/RETRIEVAL. Both THE SOURCE and COMPU-SERVE have all kinds of information, news and programs, charging about $5 an hour when you log on. Talk to some subscribers to these and other such networks to see if they have what you need.

DEAL!

I don't know whether they will still have this deal when you get your modem or communication package, but the VICMODEM included free membership in Compu-Serve and Dow Jones, plus one free hour of use. This is a good way to check out these services to see if they are what you need. If they are not, you're not out the cost of membership. So before you purchase a modem, see if they include such a deal.

Summary

The most important thing to understand from this last chapter is that we have only scratched the surface of what is available for the COMMODORE-64 computer. There is much, much more than a single chapter could possible cover and, as you come to know your COMMODORE-64, you will find that the choice of software and peripherals is limited only by the confusion in making up your mind. There were other items for the COMMODORE-64 that came to mind, but this chapter and book would have never ended were I to indulge myself and keep prattling on. The software and hardware I suggested were based on personal preferences, and I would suggest that you choose on the basis of your own needs and preferences, not mine. Think of the items mentioned as a random sampling of what one user found to be useful and then, after your own sampling, examination and testing, get exactly what *you* need.

As you end this book, you should have a beginning level understanding of your computer's ability. Whether you use it for a single function or are a dedicated hacker, it is important that you understand the scope of its capacity to help you in your work, education and play. It is not a monstrous electronic mystery, but rather a tool to help you in various ways. You may not understand exactly how it operates, but you probably do not understand everything about how your car's engine works either, and that never prevented you from driving. Furthermore, like your car, you should think of your computer as a vehicle that will take you where you want, and never again consider it a machine that you must follow.

Appendix A

Using the C-64 WEDGE

The "Test-Demo" diskette that comes with your 1541 disk drive has an excellent disk operating system that will save you a lot of time over using the method discussed in the first two chapters. First, to load the C-64 WEDGE, enter:

```
LOAD "C-64 WEDGE", 8 <RETURN>
RUN
```

Once that is done, you will have a much easier time accessing your disk. Also, you can view the disk directory without deleting the program in memory. The following is a summary of the C-64 WEDGE commands compiled by (who else) COMMODORE USERS GROUP!

LOAD	/
LOAD & RUN	↑
LOAD To Address	%
SAVE	←
SAVE and REPLACE	←@0:A
	A=Program Name
ERROR DISPLAY	@
DIRECTORY	>$ or @$
DIRECTORY for 2 Drives	@$dn
	dn= drive number
DIRECTORY for Range	@$:A
	A=alpha character
DIRECTORY for Range for 2 Drives	@$dn:A
RENAME file or program	@R0:N=O
	N=New O=Old
FORMAT disk	@N0:nm,id
	nm=Name id=Id number
SCRATCH File or Program	@S0:Pg Nm
	Pg Nm = Program Name
SCRATCH Range	@S0:fl*
	fl=first letters

The SCRATCH Range command will delete *all* disk files if you do not include the first letters. That is, if you enter @S0:*, all your programs will be creamed!

Copy File A to File B   @C0:O=0:N
                               O=old name N=new name
Reset Disk Drive   @U0
Initialize Disk   @I
Disable Wedge   @Q
Enable Wedge   SYS 52224

COMPLIMENTS OF THE COMMODORE USERS GROUP

COMMODORE-64 COMMAND EXAMPLES

This glossary is arranged in *alphabetical* order. The examples are set up to show you how to use the commands and their proper syntax. In some cases when a command has different contexts of usage, more than a single example will be used. Some examples are given in the Immediate mode and some in the Program mode <those with line numbers> and some with both. Results are given to show what a particular configuration would create in some examples for clarification. Some commands of specialized use which were not covered in the text have been included here for a more complete glossary.

ABS( ) Gives the absolute value of a number or variable.
      PRINT ABS(-123.45)
      <RESULT> 123.45

AND Logical operator used in IF/THEN statement.
      140 IF A$ < > "Y" AND A$ < > "N" THEN GOTO 100

ASC( ) Returns ASCII value of first character in string.
      PRINT ASC ("W"). or A$ = "COMMODORE-64" : PRINT ASC(A$)

ATN( ) Returns arctangent of number or variable.
      PRINT ATN (123)
      <RESULT> 1.56266643

CHR$( ) Returns the character with a given decimal value.
      PRINT CHR$(65)
      <RESULT> A

CLOSE Closes channel to device or file.
      210 CLOSE7 : REM 7 IS FILE NUMBER OF DEVICE OR FILE BEING CLOSED.

CLR All variables are reset to zero.
      120 CLR

CMD Sends output to an OPENed device or file specified by file number.
      OPEN7,4
      CMD7
      LIST

CONT Continue program after a STOP or END statement in program
      CONT

COS( ) Returns to cosine of variable or number.
```
PRINT COS(123)
<RESULTS> -.887968907
```

DATA Strings or numbers to be read with READ statement.
```
1000 DATA 2, 345, HELLO, "WALK"
```

DEF FN( ) Defines a substitute function for real variable.
```
40 DEF FN K(X) = X * X
50 PRINT FN K(4)
(Results = 16 when RUN)
```

DIM Allocates maximum range of array.
```
130 DIM A$ (100)
```

END Terminates running of program.
```
200 END
```

EXP( ) Returns $e = 2.718289$ to indicated power.
```
PRINT EXP (5)
<RESULTS> 7.69478526E+23
```

FOR Sets up beginning of FOR/NEXT loop and top limit of loop.
```
40 FOR I = 1 TO 100
```

FRE( ) Returns available memory.
```
PRINT FRE(0)
```

GET Halts execution until single entry received from keyboard.
```
30 GET A$ : IF A$ = "" THEN 30
```

GET# Inputs one character from a previously OPENed device or file.
```
GET#12, R$(I)
```

GOSUB Branches to subroutine at given line number.
```
100 GOSUB 200
```

GOTO (or GO TO) Branches to given line number.
```
100 GOTO 200
```

IF/THEN Sets up conditional logic for execution.
```
60 IF A$ = "Q" THEN END
```

INPUT Halts program execution until strings or numbers are entered and RETURN key is pressed. May enter message within INPUT statement.
```
90 INPUT "ENTER WORD-> "; W$(I)
100 INPUT "ENTER NUMBER -> "; A
110 INPUT "ENTER INTEGER NUMBER -> "; N%
120 PRINT "HIT 'RETURN' TO CONTINUE ";
130 INPUT R$
```

INPUT# Takes data from a previously OPENed file or device.
```
200 INPUT#1, R$(I)
```

INT( ) Returns the integer value of real variable or number.
```
PRINT INT (123.45)
<RESULT> 123
```

LEFT$(,) Returns specifed number of characters from a given string beginning with character at far left.
```
10 A$ = "GOODBYE"
20 PRINT LEFT$ (A$,4)
(Results = GOOD)
```

LEN Returns the length in terms of number of characters of a specified string.
```
A$ = "COMPUTER AWAY"
PRINT LEN(A$)
<RESULTS> 12
```

LIST Lists program currently in memory.
```
LIST
```

LOAD Loads program from specified device.
```
LOAD "$",8 (Loads directory from disk)
LOAD "MYPROGRAM",1 or LOAD "MYPROGRAM" (Loads program from tape.)
```

LOG( ) Returns logarithm of specifed number or variable.
```
PRINT LOG (123)
<RETURNS> 4.81218436
or
G = 123 : PRINT LOG (G)
```

MID$(, ,) Returns a portion of a string beginning with the nth number
from the left to the length of the second number.
        10 A$ = "WONDERFUL"
        20 PRINT MID$(A$,4,3)
        (Results = DER)

NEW Clears program in memory.
        NEW

NEW (DISK) Formats diskette, ERASING any programs on disk. Requires
        an OPENed channel to disk. "N" may be substituted for "NEW".
        OPEN 15,8,15
        PRINT#15, "NEW0: MYDISK,22"

NEXT Sets the top of the loop begun with FOR statement.
        10 FOR I = 1 TO 100
        20 PRINT "THIS" ,
        30 NEXT I

NOT Logical negation in IF/THEN statement.
        60 IF A NOT B THEN GOTO 100

ON Sets up computed GOTO and GOSUB.
        190 ON A GOSUB 1000,2000,3000

OPEN Opens channel to device or file.
        500 OPEN1,1,1 "NAME LIST" (Opens tape file "NAME LIST")
        OPEN7,4 (Opens channel to printer)

OR Logical OR in IF/THEN statement.
        130 IF A=10 OR B = 20 THEN GOTO 190

PEEK Returns memory contents of given decimal location.
        170 PRINT PEEK (768)
        180 IF PEEK(768) = 5 THEN GOTO 200

POKE Inserts given value in specified memory location.
        POKE 768,10 (Sets memory location 768 to decimal value 10)

POS( ) Gives the current horizontal position of the cursor.
        10 PRINT "THIS LINE";: PRINT POS(0)
        <RESULTS> THIS LINE 9

PRINT Outputs string, number or variable to screen or printer. (Can substitute "?" for PRINT.)
PRINT 1;2;3; "GO"; F$; A; N%

PRINT# Sends output to specified OPENed device or file. (The question mark (?) *cannot* be substituted when using PRINT#.)
250 PRINT#1, NA$(I)
or
OPEN7,4
PRINT#7 "HELLO COMMODORE-64"
<RESULTS> Prints message HELLO COMMODORE-64 to printer.

READ Enters DATA contents into variable.
10 READ A : READ B$
20 DATA 5, "BATS"

REM Non-executable command. Allows remarks in program lines.
10 DIM A$(122) : REM DIMENSIONS STRING ARRAY "A$" TO 122

RESTORE Resets position of READ to first DATA statement.
10 FOR I = 1 TO 5 : READ A$(I) : NEXT
20 RESTORE

RETURN Returns program to next line after GOSUB command
500 RETURN

RIGHT$ (,) Returns the rightmost n characters of given string.
10 A$ = "DATAMOST" : PRINT RIGHT$(A$,4)
(Results = MOST)

RND( ) Generates a random number less than 1 and greater than or equal to 0.
PRINT RND(5)
INT (RND (1) * (N) + 1) - Generates whole random numbers from 1 to N, with N being the upper limit of desired numbers.

RUN Executes program in memory.
RUN

SAVE Records program on tape or disk.
SAVE "GRAPH PLOT" <tape>
SAVE "GRAPH PLOT" ,1,1 <tape with end of tape marker>
SAVE "GRAPH PLOT",8 <disk>

SIN( ) Returns the sine of variable or number.
PRINT SIN(123)
<RESULTS = -.459903491>

SPC( ) Prints specified number of spaces.
PRINT SPC(29); "HERE"

SQR( ) Returns the squareroot of variable or number.
PRINT SQR(64)

STOP Halts execution and prints line number where break occurs. (CONT command will re-start program at next instruction after STOP command.)
100 STOP

STR$( ) Converts number/variable into string variable.
20 T = 123 : T$ = STR$(T) : TT$ = "$" + T$ + ".00"

SYS. Calls and executes a machine language subroutine from decimal addresses between 0 and 65535.
SYS 58692 <CLEARS SCREEN AND HOMES CURSOR>
10 FOR I = 1 TO 800: PRINT "X"; : NEXT
20 FOR I = 1 TO 20 : SYS 59626 : NEXT
<RESULTS> Prints 800 "X's" on the screen and then scrolls (SYS 59626) 20 times.

TAB( ) Sets horizontal tab from within a PRINT statement.
PRINT TAB(20);"HERE"

TAN( ) Provides the tangent of number or variable.
40 T = 34 : V = 55
50 R = T + V : PRINT TAN(R)

VAL( ) Used to convert string to numeric value.
30 H$ = "123" : PRINT VAL(H$)

SCREEN DISPLAY CODES

SET 1	SET 2	POKE	SET 1	SET 2	POKE	SET 1	SET 2	POKE
@		0	£		28	8		56
A	a	1	]		29	9		57
B	b	2	↑		30	:		58
C	c	3	←		31	;		59
D	d	4	SPACE		32	<		60
E	e	5	!		33	=		61
F	f	6	"		34	>		62
G	g	7	#		35	?		63
H	h	8	$		36	[graphic]		64
I	i	9	%		37	[graphic]	A	65
J	j	10	&		38	[graphic]	B	66
K	k	11	'		39	[graphic]	C	67
L	l	12	(		40	[graphic]	D	68
M	m	13	)		41	[graphic]	E	69
N	n	14	*		42	[graphic]	F	70
O	o	15	+		43	[graphic]	G	71
P	p	16	,		44	[graphic]	H	72
Q	q	17	−		45	[graphic]	I	73
R	r	18	.		46	[graphic]	J	74
S	s	19	/		47	[graphic]	K	75
T	t	20	0		48	[graphic]	L	76
U	u	21	1		49	[graphic]	M	77
V	v	22	2		50	[graphic]	N	78
W	w	23	3		51	[graphic]	O	79
X	x	24	4		52	[graphic]	P	80
Y	y	25	5		53	[graphic]	Q	81
Z	z	26	6		54	[graphic]	R	82
[		27	7		55	[graphic]	S	83

SET 1	SET 2	POKE	SET 1	SET 2	POKE	SET 1	SET 2	POKE
	T	84			99			102
	U	85			100			103
	V	86			101			104
	W	87			105			117
	X	88			106			118
	Y	89			107			119
	Z	90			108			120
		91			109			121
		92			110		✓	122
		93			111			123
		94			112			124
		95			113			125
SPACE		96			114			126
		97			115			127
		98			116			

INDEX